Options Trading Crash Course

How to Start in Options Trading and How to Create Passive Income Using Simple Strategies (Beginner Friendly).

I0499908

Ben Price

Table of Contents

Introduction

Chapter 1: An Overview of the Options Trading

What is an option?
The strike price
Expiration date
Options pricing
Total loss
Types of options: call option, put option, European style options
Opening and closing position
Option premium
The long call strategy: basic idea
The long put strategy: basic idea
Break-even prices
The origin of option names
Leaps
What is a liquid asset
The market maker
Options Clearing Corporation
Options Industry Council
How risky are options?

Chapter 2: How to Trade Options

Selecting a brokerage
How much money do I need to start?
Should I open a margin account?
Day trading

A list of brokerages
Reading Options Chains
Bid and ask
Volume and open interest
Options trading levels
Taxes and options profits

Chapter 3: Advantages of Trading Options

Options provide leverage
Options are inexpensive
Options prices change in big way
Options have a higher ROI
Options are flexible
Options are fast

Chapter 4: Buying and Selling Options

Can you make profits buying call options?
Never let an option run to expiration
Set a cutoff to exit your trade
Pay attention
Become familiar with limit orders and use them
Follow trends
Buying multiple contracts
How many different stocks?
Picking your expiration date
Buy out of the money or in the money?
Put options
Basic trading: summary

Chapter 5: Options Strategies Part 1

Assignment risk
Debit spreads
Put debit spread
Strangle
Straddle
Earnings calls

Chapter 6: Options Strategies Part 2

Put credit spread
Time frames
Sell out of the money for low risk
What happens if the price heads south?
Call credit spread
Iron condor
Summary

Chapter 7: Selling Options as a Strategy

Covered calls
Protected put
Put options as insurance
Selling naked puts
Selling naked call options

Chapter 8: Avoiding Beginner Mistakes and Tips

Panicking and exiting early
Getting involved in many trades at once
Using too many strategies

Taking too much risk
Set it and forget it
Forgetting about time decay
When selling options, stop looking at probabilities
Not paying attention to volatility
Not having a training plan
Not giving enough time or even thinking about time

Conclusion

Introduction

If you've been researching on investing online lately, I'm sure you've been hearing a lot about options. You've probably seen a lot of fancy gurus offering to sell you an expensive course, where they'll give you their latest picks for only $1,495. But let me save you the trouble. Everything they're going to teach you in those courses is available right here in this book. You can also get a lot of free resources online through YouTube videos that will teach you all you need to know about options.

In this book, we are going to explain what options are and how they are traded on the markets. First, we're going to cover buying and trading options. This is where the vast majority of people are going to be getting started when investing in options. One of the first things you need to know about options is that they are regulated a little bit more than stocks are. So what you can do with the options is going to be a little bit limited in the beginning. But as you get experience, the broker will allow you to enter more trades. The reason that options are regulated is that there are some complicated ways that options can be traded. The SEC and brokerage firms don't want amateurs trying to enter into those complicated trading schemes without gaining some experience first. In addition, if you are writing options contracts–don't worry if you don't understand what that means right now we will talk about that in the book –there is some risk that you are going to have to buy or sell 100 shares of stock. So you either have to have the capital on hand to satisfy that requirement or have a margin account. However, no need to worry, as we will give you the strategies that you can use to avoid getting in that situation in this book. And please note that if you just go in the market and buy an option to sell it later for a profit, this situation doesn't apply.

After we cover the basics of buying and selling options, we're going to talk about some of the strategies that can be used to increase the odds of making a profit, and also look at some things that you simply can't do using stocks. For example, you can set up options trades that will make profits no matter which direction the stock moves. We will also discuss some unique setups using options that are extremely low risk that can allow you to earn a regular income on the stock market without even owning any assets. This may not make sense right now but by the end of the book, you will have a solid understanding of these topics.

One of the best things about investing in options is the fact that you don't need all that much money to get started. If you are careful you can start with a few hundred dollars and grow it to a few thousand dollars in no time. There are a few key reasons why most people fail to do this, and we will be covering these in the book. Of course, I can't be there when you actually enter your trades, so it's up to you heed the advice given in this book that's a follow it carefully. So let's go ahead and get started and learn what options are all about.

Chapter 1: An Overview of the Options Trading

In this chapter, we are going to introduce the concept of options. We are going to explain what they are, the different types of options that are available, and explain how to get started in options trading. One of the best things about options is that you can literally get started with just $20, $50, or $100. You don't have to be rich to trade options and you don't have to have access to a lot of liquid capital. So despite their glorified reputation in the perception that they are very sophisticated, options trading is really something that's accessible to anyone who wants to try it.

There is only one drawback with options. When you trade options, this is not like investing in a mutual fund. It's also not like buying stocks for the traditional buy-and-hold philosophy. Trading options is something that requires active involvement in your trading activities. So you're going to have to pay fairly close attention to what's going on with your trades. You also have to be ready to enter and exit trades at the right moments.

What is an Option?

An option is a contract on 100 shares of stock which are referred to as the underlying. The contract enables the purchaser to either buy or sell 100 shares of stock at a fixed price. Each option comes with an expiration date. Typically, an options contract last for about a month. These usually expire on the third Friday of every month; but there are also options contracts that only last for one week, and there are others that last for long time periods, from 1 to 2 years. But when you start looking into options you're going to see that when it comes to the popular stocks like Amazon and Facebook or the stock indexes, there are options available with virtually any expiration date you desire. For individual stocks what I actually mean by this is that you can find a Friday expiration date to your liking. Some of the more popular index funds have options that expire every few days. Later on, we will see the best ways to choose your expiration dates.

The Strike Price

The fixed price that is used to buy or sell the underlying shares is called the *strike price*. The value of the strike price is the entire reason that options have value in the marketplace. The strike price is only part of the options contract, the shares of the underlying stock are being traded on the market at the current share price. However, if the option contract is actually exercised, the shares of stock would be bought or sold at the strike price and not using the market price of the shares. This can allow traders to buy shares of stock at a steep discount, or to sell them for a profit in a bear market. However, as an options trader, you are not going to be interested in buying or selling the shares of stock. Your goal is to profit either by selling options or by trading them when you can buy and sell at a profit.

Expiration Date

One of the most important concepts that a new options trader needs to come to grips with is the fact that options come with an expiration date. This is very different than investing in stocks which basically have an unlimited lifetime. The expiration date has major implications for the way that options work, and this will impact you whether or not you are simply buying options to trade or selling them in the marketplace. We will be discussing the expiration date extensively in this book, and talk about strategies that you can use to benefit from the expiration date. Keep in mind that one of the biggest pitfalls for beginners is ignoring the expiration date. A beginner will buy an option to trade, and maybe the trade doesn't go as expected, but they hold on hoping for a recovery in the future. That's a natural way to look at things if you are coming at options from the perspective of trading stocks. But what often happens, is the trader comes back to see how their option is doing, and they find out it's lost a lot of its value. So a small loss the trader has incurred due to changing stock prices gets magnified into a large loss because the option is about to expire. We'll be emphasizing avoiding getting in this situation in this book.

Options Pricing

When you are just getting started, it's important to become acquainted with options pricing. Options prices are quoted on a per-share basis. But the actual price you have to pay to buy the option is for 100 shares. So if you see an option with a quoted price of $2.50, that means to buy it you actually have to pay $2.50 x 100 = $250. We will explore the way that you read a traditional options chain later, but most brokerages give simple price quotes these days in a mobile application or on their website without using the complicated strings from options chains. Options will be sorted by expiration date, so you'll first select the expiration date you are interested in. Then they will be listed in order by strike price. You will see the per-share cost of the option listed for each strike price.

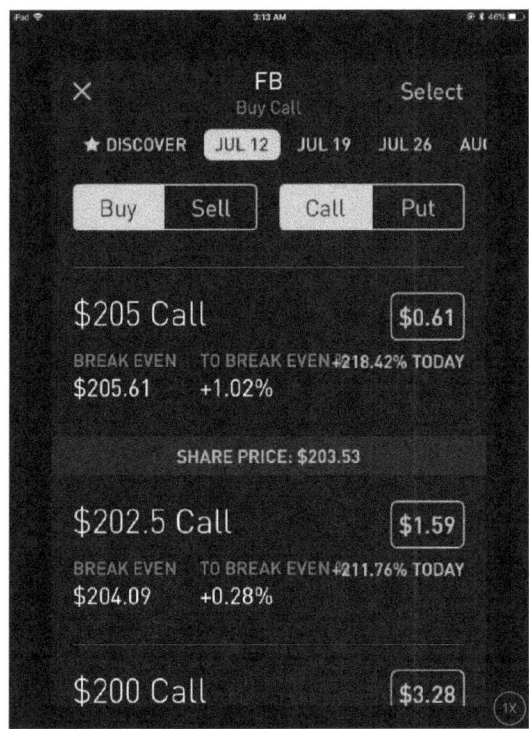

Total Loss

The maximum loss that you can incur with an option is the price you paid to buy it. So if you purchased an option on AMD for $35 and it doesn't work out, the maximum loss you will incur is $35. Options prices vary widely, an option on Apple might cost around $200, while an option on Amazon might cost $4,700. But no matter which option you purchase, the purchase price is the maximum loss. You should never get into a situation where you take the maximum loss, but a lot of naïve traders actually end up in that position.

Types of Options

There are two types of options. An option is either a *call* option or a *put* option. Let's explore each of these in turn, and see why you'd want to invest in either one.

Call Option

If you buy a call option, this gives you the option to purchase 100 shares of the underlying stock at the strike price. The strike price is a fixed quantity for the lifetime of the options contract. So if the strike price is $88, but the stock rises to $275 in the market, it doesn't matter. If the option hasn't expired you can buy the shares at $88 a share. But doing so is "optional". You are not in any way shape or form required to actually buy the shares of stock.

If the price of the shares on the market goes up, then the value of the option goes up and you can sell it for a profit. On the other hand, if the price of the shares goes down, you will lose money. We will be talking about how to handle this when we discuss profiting with options.

The relationship of the strike price to the market price is one of the most important qualities of an option. For a call option, if the strike price is lower than the market price, that is a huge advantage to the buyer, since it enables them to buy 100 shares of stock at a discount. For that reason, if the strike price is lower than the market price for a call option, we say that it's *in the money*.

If the strike price is above the market price of the shares, then the ability to buy the shares at the strike price is worthless. For this reason, we say that the option is *out of the money* in this circumstance. These options will still have some value if the share price is below the strike price, depending on the time remaining to expiration. The reason is that time gives the stock price a chance to move enough so that the option will go in the money.

If the strike price is exactly equal to share price, then we say the option is *at the money*. It's not common for the share price to be exactly equal to the strike price, but it can happen for short periods.

Since a call option increases in value when the strike price is below the share price on the market, when you buy a call option you are hoping for the share price to rise. So you're taking a traditional bullish position. When you buy a call option we say that you are *long* on the call option. When you hear the jargon "long" that just means that you opened your position by purchasing (buying) the option.

Put Option

A put option is a little bit different for most investors. If you aren't a big trader, you probably haven't been going around shorting stock. So you aren't used to thinking in terms of hoping for a market decline. Normally, that is the purview of traders who have a large number of resources. You might imagine big hedge funds shorting stock, and making profits when the price declines.

A put option gives you the right to sell 100 shares of stock at the strike price.

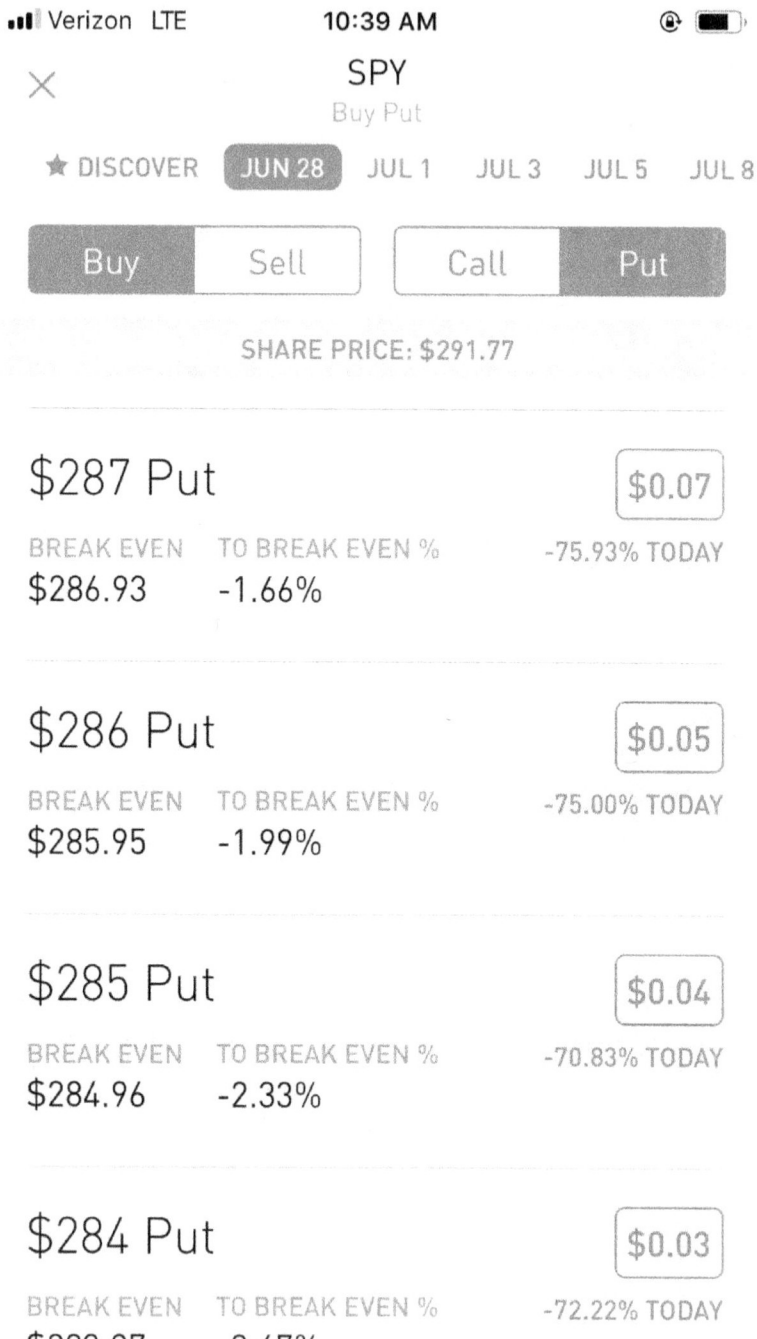

★ DISCOVER   **JUN 28**   JUL 1   JUL 3   JUL 5   JUL 8

| Buy | Sell | | Call | Put |

SHARE PRICE: $291.77

$287 Put $0.07

BREAK EVEN   TO BREAK EVEN %   -75.93% TODAY
$286.93   -1.66%

$286 Put $0.05

BREAK EVEN   TO BREAK EVEN %   -75.00% TODAY
$285.95   -1.99%

$285 Put $0.04

BREAK EVEN   TO BREAK EVEN %   -70.83% TODAY
$284.96   -2.33%

$284 Put $0.03

BREAK EVEN   TO BREAK EVEN %   -72.22% TODAY
$283.97   -2.67%

Put options enable small investors like us to get in on this kind of action. So a put option works in the opposite way as compared to a call option, it gains in value when the stock price declines. The more the stock price declines, the more money you make. Put options can be used for some interesting strategies that we will explore later on, either alone or in combination with call options.

So a put option has the most value if the strike price is higher than the market price of the stock. If the strike price of a put option is $90, but the market price of the stock is $100, the put option won't be worth exercising, since you could sell the shares on the open market at a higher price. But if the share price drops to $70 a share, then the option becomes worth a lot more. That's because you can buy the shares on the market at $70 a share, and then sell them at the strike price of $90 a share, earning a $20 a share profit.

As an options trader, you're probably never going to do that, however. The goal with put options is to buy them when the price is relatively low, and then sell them when the price goes up during a bear market.

Now let's talk about the relationship between the strike price of a put option and the market price of the stock. If the share price of the stock is higher than the strike price of the put option, we say that the put option is out of the money. If the share price of the stock is equal to the strike price of the put option, then it's at the money. Finally, if the share price of the stock drops below the strike price, the option is in the money.

Out of the money put options still have some value, because there is a chance that they will move in the money because the stock price drops before the option expires. The further away from the expiration date is, the higher the probability is that this will happen at some point. That means that out of the money options that are further away from the expiration date will have more value than out of the money options that are close to the expiration date.

Although a put option is equivalent to "shorting" the stock, because you are hoping that the price of the shares is going to drop, we say that you are *long* on a put option if you buy it.

European Style Options

Some options are "American Style" and some options are "European Style". Most options in the United States, as you might guess are American style. That means that they can be exercised on or before the expiration date. European style options can only be exercised on the expiration date. The differences between the two option types are important when you are implementing options strategies that earn income. There are some European style options you can trade in the United States. The most popular of these are on indexes, including SPX, which is the S & P 500 index, RUT, which is the Russell 3000 index, and NDX, which is an index of the top 103 stocks on NASDAQ. Not all trading platforms allow you to trade these options, please check with your brokerage. Major stocks in individual companies like Facebook, Google, or Apple are American style options.

Opening and Closing a Position

If you are new to trading, it's important to take a moment to familiarize yourself with some more jargon in the industry. When you buy an option, you are opening a position. We also say that you are entering the position. However, we say the same thing if you start by selling an option. So if you buy the option, we say that you buy to open. If you are selling an option to start, we say that you are selling to open. Many introductory options treatments discuss 'writing' an options contract, and someone wrote the options contracts that you see being traded on the exchange. However, as a small ("retail") investor, you are not going to actually write options contracts. What you can do, is you can pick one that is already in existence, and sell it to open. Selling options is more complicated than simply buying them and trading them for a profit, so we'll be talking about that a little bit later.

When you are buying an option to open or enter the position, then to get out of or exit the position, you sell the option. So you "sell to close". This is the common-sense notion of buying and selling that you are used to.

If you sell an option to open your position, you can buy it back to exit the position. So the lingo here is you "buy to close". The thing about options is you don't have to buy the exact contract back, you only have to buy one with the same terms to get out of the position.

Luckily there are usually thousands of them on the market for high-interest stocks. But knowing how many are available is something important that we'll get into later.

So if you buy a call option to open the position, you are long on the call. If you buy a put option, you are long on the put. Or we can refer to these as the long call and the long put. In contrast, if you sell a call option to open the position, it's a short call. Similarly selling a put option to open the position is a short put.

Option Premium

The price paid to buy the option is called the *premium.* You are probably familiar with insurance premiums, and the fact that the same name is used is not an accident. As we'll see later, options are a kind of insurance on stocks. If you sell to open a position, we say that you are *selling premium.* If you buy to open an options contract, the premium is just the price you paid to buy the contract on the exchange.

The Long Call Strategy: Basic Idea

The basic idea for the long call strategy is simple. You buy a call option at a desirable price when you hope the price of the stock is going to rise in value in the near future. In most cases, this is going to be a short time period. It can be a week, a month, or 45 days. You can also do this over a longer time frame from a couple of months out to two years before expiration. But the further you go out with the expiration date, the more the option is going to cost.

If a call option is in the money, the higher the share price goes the "deeper" in the money the option is. The deeper in the money, the more the option is going to be worth.

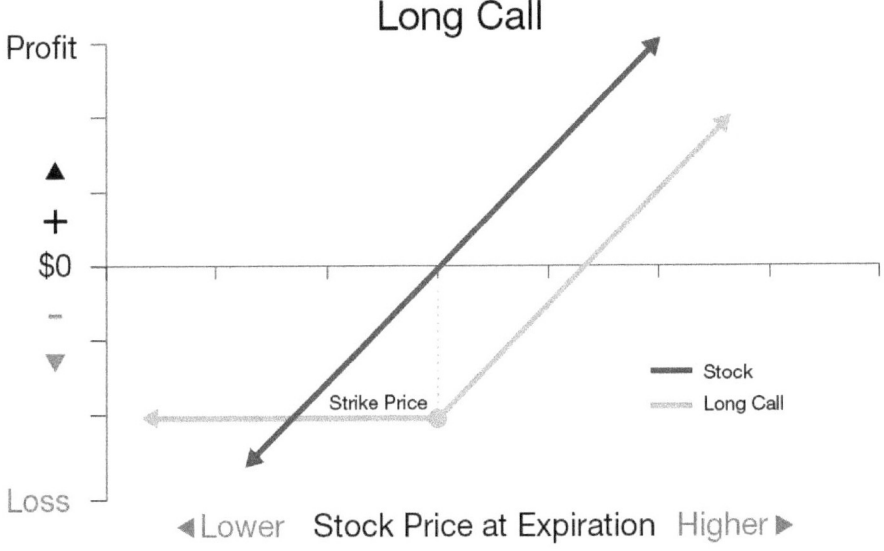

Long Call

When the price of the stock rises, your option will increase in value. At that point, you can sell the option for a profit. Of course, it's not that simple, but that is our goal when using the strategy. We will discuss how it works in practice later.

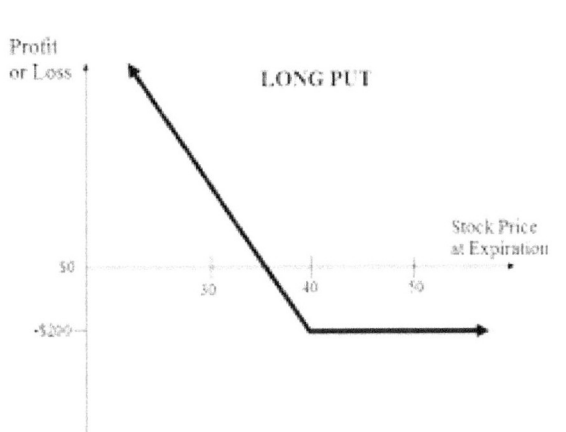

The Long Put Strategy: Basic Idea

You buy a put option when you are expecting the

27

price of a stock drop in the near future. For beginners, this can be hard to wrap your mind around. But keep in mind what an explosive strategy this is. While your friends can only invest in stocks with the hope that the price of the shares will rise when you're investing in options you are in a market where you can make money either way. So if there is an indication that the stock is going to drop in price, you can buy a put option. The options available are going to follow the same patterns that we saw with call options, and so you'll be able to find options that expire in a few days, in a week, a month, 45 days and so on. Just like with call options, the value of a put option increases in value the further away it is from the expiration date. That's because more time means a higher probability that at some point the price of the stock is going to move in such a way that the put option goes in the money, or goes "deeper" in the money. When a put option is deeper in the money, that means that the share price is lower with respect to the strike price of the option than it had been previously.

Break-Even Prices

Options are always quoted with a break-even price. This is a pretty straightforward concept, but let's start with a call option. The break-even price is the price that the market price of the share would have to be in order to make it worth it for a buyer to exercise the option and buy the shares. That price is going to be the strike price plus the price paid for the option on a per-share basis.

If the price of the option is $1, and the strike price of the call option is $198, then the break-even price is $1 + $198 = $199. That means to break even the share price has to rise to $199. If the share price rises to $198.50, it's true that the option is in the money. But it's not worth exercising and buying the shares, because if you buy the shares you are stuck with the $1 per share you paid for the option. So you'd save $0.50 by being able to buy the shares at $198, but that is wiped out by the $0.50 leftover from buying the option. The share price has to rise to $199 in order to completely account for the money paid to buy the option.

When you are selling options (that is sell to open your position) the break-even price is important to know. Your concern when selling options contracts is that the buyer will exercise the option if it goes in the money. So it's important to know what the break-even price of any option you sell is because it's not going to be exercised unless the price moves enough that it goes above the break-even price for a call. Otherwise, there is no advantage to the buyer.

For a put option, you get the break-even price by subtracting the price of the option from the strike price. So the market price of the stock has to go below the break-even price to make it worthwhile for the buyer to exercise the option. Using our previous example, if you buy an option for $1 a share and the strike price is $198, the break-even price is $198 - $1 = $197.

The Origin of Option Names

Just for the record, the name *call* means that if you sell to open a call option, you can have the shares "called away", that is you have to sell them to an options buyer if they decide to exercise the contract. A *put* means that if you sell to open a put option, you might have the stock "put to you", that is you'll have to buy the shares. While the terms of an option are "optional" for anyone who buys to open a position, if you sell to open a position you must follow the terms outlined in the contract if it is exercised.

Leaps

A *LEAP* is a long-term equity anticipation security. Actually, there is nothing special about a LEAP. It's just an option that expires 1-2 years in the future. Since there is a long time before expiration, they cost a lot more to buy. However, you can make great profits from leaps and use them in different strategies.

What is a Liquid Asset?

Just to make sure that everyone is on board with financial jargon, you need to understand what a liquid asset is. In general, a liquid asset is one that can be quickly converted into cash. Cash is obviously 100% liquid. A house isn't very liquid, because in most markets it would take time to sell it. If an asset isn't very liquid, you can say it's *illiquid*. A car is more liquid than a house. It's still not that liquid. A bar of gold is more liquid than a car in most circumstances.

When it comes to options, the liquidity of the option is an important concept. If you are going to be a successful options trader, in most cases you're going to want to invest in liquid options. When it comes to the liquidity of options we are interested in how long it's going to take to buy and sell the option. This is important because in some cases you are going to want to enter and exit trades quickly. If there isn't much interest in an option, it might take a long time to find someone to sell it at a price you want to pay, and if you are selling it, you might not be able to find a buyer fast. Finding a buyer fast is important if there are large moves brewing in the market. You might be in a position where you want to get out before you incur losses, or you might be selling in order to take profits. If it's an option that doesn't have a large number of people who are interested in holding it, it might be hard to sell the option. If you are at a level where you earned profits but the option isn't liquid, you might find that you are unable to sell it at the right time, and you'll be stuck, possibly even moving into a losing position. This is important if you sell to open as well. As we will see later in the book, if you sell to open, you might have to buy the option back. If the option isn't very liquid, you might find yourself in a serious bind, and be forced to keep your position open. That could have major consequences.

The options that are going to have the most liquidity are those that have major stocks like Netflix, GM, Apple, Amazon, United Healthcare and other big companies as the underlying. Index funds are also excellent, in fact, some of the hottest trades in the options market are with index funds. In the next chapter, we will show you how to determine whether or not an option has enough liquidity.

The Market Maker

In your day-to-day trading, you don't really need to know what the market maker is, but in order to be educated, it's good to have some idea of what that is about. Market Markers are large traders who maintain big portfolios of options contracts. It used to be more common for market makers to be high net-worth individuals, but now most market makers are associated with big institutions like banks. The market maker actually serves a purpose on the options markets. They are there to keep the markets liquid. That doesn't mean they are going to buy any old option, the market maker maintains their own portfolio in order to make profits. But if you are selling an option that is hard to get rid of but it's one they are interested in, they'll buy the option. Alternatively, you might be able to buy an option from the market maker in circumstances where it might be difficult to find a seller.

However, when you are actually trading options, you are not going to have any idea whatsoever who you are trading with. You simply place your buy and sell orders with a brokerage, and they are executed or they expire. You might be selling an option to a market maker, another retail/individual investor, the manager of a hedge fund, or an institutional investor. You don't know who it is and it really doesn't matter. There isn't any direct negotiation, although we will talk about pricing your orders in the next chapter to facilitate fast transactions.

Options Clearing Corporation

Options markets are managed in part by the Options Clearing Corporation or OCC. This organization is based in Chicago, IL. One of the roles played by the OCC is to keep options markets stable. It manages options and also futures contracts. The OCC is the guarantor of options contracts. This means that it will fulfill the role required under the obligations of an option (buy or sell stock) if the originator of the option is unable to do so. This helps keep the market stable since people that exercise options are buying them with the expectation that the terms of the contract are carried out as specified. If that didn't happen, the market would fall apart since people wouldn't be assured of having the terms met.

Options Industry Council

The options industry council, or OIC, is an organization dedicated to the options markets. Its role is primarily an educational one, and it strives to educate the public on how options work, and what the risks of trading options are.

How Risky Are Options?

First, let's be clear. Any investment of any kind carries risk with it. You are always at risk of losing your entire investment, whether you are buying gold, cryptocurrency, stocks, or options.

In the case of options, your maximum loss when buying an option is the price you paid for the option. We will see later that losses get a little more complicated when you use advanced options strategies, however, the risk is always a fixed amount.

It's possible to be foolish and lose on all of your trades. However, if you are careful and make smart moves, options trading isn't that hard to profit from. You can even be in a situation where you are just breaking even if you are following some simple principles of caution that we are going to discuss throughout the book. I hate to be blunt, but only a total fool loses all of their money trading options.

Chapter 2: How to Trade Options

Now we have an overview of the basics of options trading. It's time to get down in the ditches and start getting dirty. The first step is to understand the mechanics of buying and selling options. In this chapter, we are going to discuss how to set up a brokerage account, how much money you need, and how to go about placing trades. We aren't going to talk about making profitable trades yet, but we are going to look at some characteristics of options that you need to pay attention to when you are trading.

Selecting a **Brokerage**

The first step in your journey to becoming an options trader to open a brokerage account. Maybe you already have one buying and investing in stocks. If you do then there probably isn't anything extra that you need to take care of. But there are a few things you need to consider before you stick with it or use a particular broker.

The first item of importance to consider is the level of options trading that you plan to be involved with. In the event that you are only going to be buying and selling options, that is *trading* them, you don't need to worry too much about the capabilities offered by the broker. The one worry that may come up is when you have the intention of doing what's called *selling naked*. We are going to get into this later but the idea of selling naked means selling options contracts with nothing to back them. Although it sounds really risky, it's not as risky as people make it out to be, as long as it's handled correctly. The reason this is an issue is that some brokers may not allow naked selling of options.

For all other types of options trading, including implementing advanced strategies that we will discuss in this book, the vast majority of brokerage firms are more than adequate. The issue then becomes commissions that are charged trading options. You need to know the exact amounts a brokerage charges for commissions, and also check to see if they are quoting it per trade or per share. Remember that an options contract is 100 shares, so if someone tells you its $0.05, then it's $5 per contract. Furthermore, you need to know what the commission charged for options is - don't confuse that with commissions that they charge for buying and selling *stocks*.

For beginners, one of the best options trading platforms the *Robin Hood* app which is available in the Apple App Store and on Google play as well. Robin Hood is very easy to use for trading options. One of the best features of Robin Hood is the fact that it doesn't have commissions. That is trading on Robin Hood is commission-free. With options in particular, and if your trading frequently, that could be important for your bottom line. Older and more established brokerages will try to dissuade you from using a commission-free platform like Robin Hood. It is true that Robin Hood has its drawbacks, but they don't necessarily outweigh the benefits. The main problem with Robin Hood is that it lacks many of the evaluation tools that some of the bigger and more established brokerages you may have access to. However, I have found in my trading that having access to those tools the brokerage is not really necessary. One reason it's not necessary is that you have access to all those tools on the Internet at large, and all the tools you need are free of charge. The first thing you should do if you're not doing it already is to familiarize yourself with the *Yahoo finance* website. You can find everything there you need in order to evaluate stocks to make profitable trades.

The main thing that you want to learn how to use on Yahoo finance is the charting tool. So my advice for beginners getting started is to first learn your way around the Yahoo finance website. And focus on using the charts to examine the trends of stocks you are interested in. This will include knowing how to view a candlestick chart and adding indicators to the chart. In particular, you are going to want to add moving averages to your chart. So before you get started trading make sure that you know how to do this.

Of course Robin Hood is not the only possibility for trading options. *Tasty works* is a highly regarded website and brokerage for trading options, especially if you plan to sell naked. They do charge commissions, visit their website so that you can know what the commissions are and evaluate the situation yourself. You should also check out their educational arm, tasty trade, which has a lot of educational videos.

Research around the Internet will reveal some other brokerage firms that don't charge commissions for trading options. The best thing to do is to look around and find one that you're comfortable with using. If you have Yahoo finance at your disposal and remember it's free of charge, then you won't necessarily need all the bells and whistles that are available from different websites. But when it comes down to it the choice of brokerage is a personal decision. So the only thing you really need to worry about is whether or not the brokerage actually allows you to trade options. The vast majority of them do, so that should not be an issue. And second, make sure that if they are charging commissions, they are not large enough to eat into your profits.

How much money do I need to start?

You don't need very much money in order to start trading options. In the beginning (if you have never done it before), I recommend that you start off only trading one option at a time. This way you can learn how it works through actual experience without risking very much money. My advice for beginners is to put $200 in your account to get started. In later chapters, we will talk about what to do with that money. For now, the only issue is setting everything up so you can begin trading. With $200 you'll be able to buy some options and hopefully, you can sell them and start growing your account with a profit. As you become more experienced and get involved with the more advanced trading strategies, then you can deposit more money into your account.

Should I open a margin account?

If you aren't familiar with it, a margin account is a special type of account set up with a broker that allows you to borrow money or shares from the broker. The law requires that you deposit $2000 in order to open a margin account. When trading stocks a margin account will give you leverage to buy twice as many stocks as you can afford with cash. But you have to keep in mind that you owe the broker money. In the case of options, requirements are a little bit different. After you have signed up with a brokerage account and find options that you're interested in trading, you should look at options check to see what the maintenance requirement is. Usually, it's 25% but you have to check with your broker to see what the actual number is, and it might vary from stock to stock. That will be an important number to know if you are using leverage in any way, including selling naked.

Day Trading

It's important to familiarize yourself with the rules that are in place for a practice known as *day trading*. A day trade is one that involves entering a position and exiting the *same* position on the same trading day. So if I buy 10 shares of Apple in the morning, and then sell the 10 shares of Apple in the afternoon, I've completed one day trade. If I buy 10 shares of Apple but hold them overnight before selling them, so sell them at market open the following day, that does not count as a day trade.

Day trading rules apply to options as well, so it's important that you keep track of any day trades that you make. Also, note that options are individual financial securities. So if you have options on Amazon, one that expires on July 19 with a strike price of $1,995 is a different financial security than an option that expires on July 19 with a strike price of $1,997. It's also a different financial security than an option that expires on July 26, but has the same strike price of $1,995. A call option that has a strike price of $1,995 and expires on July 19 is a different security than a put option that has a strike price of $1,995 and expires on July 19.

You can buy and sell as many different options on the same day as you please, but if you buy and sell the same option on one trading day that is a day trade.

If you complete 4-day trades within a 5-day trading period, your broker will designate you as a day trader. This is an important rule. For one thing, it means that you will be required to deposit $25,000 in your account. If you are unable to do so, you'll have to check with your broker to see how the situation is handled. You may be suspended for a period of time or have your account closed.

Because day trading stocks is a highly risky activity, it's heavily regulated by the Securities and Exchange Commission (SEC). Day trading options does not carry the same risk. When you are day trading stocks, you might have thousands or tens of thousands on the line, but that is probably not the case for retail options traders. Furthermore, there are technical reasons why people day trade stocks and don't hold positions overnight. You can hold positions overnight with options. You will lose some value with time decay, however. But it's nothing like day trading stocks, where you can have your account wiped out.

So, it's important to be aware that regardless of the facts, day trades of options contracts are considered day trading. So the most you can do is three per week. Sometimes day trading is an important skill to have, especially when a stock is really on the move. Your brokerage will keep track of your day trades for you in the account details.

A List of Brokerages

This is only a partial listing, but it will give you some idea of where to start. You can find these online, or in app stores for mobile phones or both.

- Ally Invest ($4.95 per trade)
- Charles Schwab($4.95 per trade)
- option ($3 per trade)

- E-Trade (charges $6.95 per trade)
- Interactive Brokers ($0.01 per share, 100 shares = $1)
- Robinhood (zero commissions- so $0 per trade)
- Tasty Works
- TD Ameritrade ($6.95 per trade)
- Trade Station ($5 per trade)
- Zacks ($0.01 per share, 100 shares = $1)

Reading Options Chains

Options have tickers, but they are kind of cryptic when you are new to the business. We can quickly learn how to read them, however. Here is an example:

SPY190717C00286000

The leading characters in the string tell you the ticker for the stock that underlies the option. In this case, it's SPY, an exchange-traded fund that follows the S & P 500.

The next two digits after the ticker are the year, in this case, 2019. This is followed by the month and day of expiration. So this option expires on July 17, 2019.

The letter in the middle will identify the option as a call(C) or a put (P).

The remaining digits identify the strike price of the option. Three decimal places are used, so the strike price of this option is $286.

Bid and Ask

When you are making trades, you're going to want to know what the bid and ask are. *Bid* is the going price that people are willing to pay to buy an option. *Ask* is the average price that people are currently asking to sell an option. You will also see the *Mark* listed, this is just the market price, the actual price where trades are occurring. If you are selling an option and need a quick sale, you can set the price to the Bid value. If you are buying an option, you may as well do it at the market price, or if you are willing to wait you can try doing it at the bid price. But keep in mind that options prices can change very fast. So if you are trying to buy an option that is increasing in value, if you wait around it might be getting pretty expensive to buy it, and by that time people aren't going to be interested in selling at your price. If you submit an order and it sits around without being executed, that is a sign that your offer is way off current market conditions.

One thing to notice is the bid-ask spread. If it's large, that can indicate there isn't much interest in the option. That may be mean it's hard to get in or out of your positions quickly.

Volume and Open Interest

Volume and open interest are good indicators that will tell you the level of trading activity going on with a particular option. Each option has its own volume and open interest, so if you check an Apple $205 option and it has particular values, that means nothing as far as the other Apple options. The Apple $204.50 option will have its own values for volume and open interest.

Open interest is the total number of contracts that are out there. This number is dynamic. If someone sells to open an option, that increases the open interest by 1. But if they buy it back, that will reduce the open interest by 1.

You want to make sure the open interest number is high enough so that you can exit your positions quickly if need be. The minimum value you should see for open interest in an option you are interested in is 100. However, when you look at the big stocks and index funds, the numbers are going to be much higher. They can range into the thousands and as high as 15,000 for a single option contract. This indicates that an option is in very high demand, and that is a very good option to get involved in trading with.

Volume is the number of trades that occurred on the particular trading day that you are looking at, or the most recent trading day if you are looking on a holiday or weekend.

There may be occasions when you trade low volume options. The stock might be moving quickly in a trend one way or the other, and you want to get in on the action. The problem with this move is you might not be able to sell it until the price has decreased. You want a high volume, high-interest stock like Facebook so that you can sell an option you want to get rid of quickly.

Options Trading Levels

You can't just walk in from the street and trade options. You have to get approval through your broker. This is done through a simple interviewing procedure. You need to tell the broker that you are interested in speculating and that you have a short time horizon.

There are four levels of options traders. Each level can do everything the level below it is allowed to do and obtaining approval to trade at a higher- level means that you will be able to enter into new types of trades. The levels are:

- Level 1: The most basic level. You can only sell covered calls and protected puts. We will discuss these later, but these are options you can sell backed by collateral (shares of stock) or cash.
- Level 2: A level 2 options trader can trade puts and calls, as long as they buy to open their position (but, they can sell covered calls and protected puts).
- Level 3: A level 3 options trader can use options trading strategies to minimize risk or to earn

income. These include selling credit spreads, buying debit spreads, buying strangles and straddles, and selling iron condors.

- Level 4: A level 4 trader can sell naked, which means they can sell options without having any collateral or cash. Actually, that isn't really true, you have to have a margin account to sell naked, and there has to be a certain level of cash in the account to cover the sale. It's a fraction of what you would need to sell a protected put, but you still need cash on hand as insurance.

Taxes and Options Profits

Options have a time-limited expiration date. So unless you invest in a LEAP and you hold it for more than one year, any profits you get from trading options are going to be short-term capital gains. The bottom line is that you're not going to get any tax benefits from this (of course it's income from doing very little and its fun, so there are obvious benefits). So in other words, the income you make from options is just ordinary income.

Unless you set up a company to own your options and do the trades, you're probably not going to be able to deduct expenses related to your options trading. So you'll just report your profits, and then add them to your ordinary income and pay the taxes owed.

Chapter 3: Advantages of Trading Options

It's useful to know why we are trading options in the first place. The fact that they are cheap, is only one factor to consider. In this chapter, we are going to look at some of the specific benefits that come with trading options. Knowing what they are is going to help you make the right investment decisions.

Options Provide Leverage

When you buy an options contract, you control 100 shares of stock for the lifetime of that option. The option is a tool that allows you to control those shares of stock without paying the full price for them. For example, Apple may be trading at $200 a share. An options contract on Apple might cost $125 for a particular strike price. Had I actually purchased the shares, the cost would be $200/share x 100 shares = $20,000. So for 0.625% of the price of the shares, I can control the shares for the time until the options contract either expires or I sell it.

Options are Inexpensive

OK, this is kind of a restatement of the point above, but to buy shares you need a lot of money. Yes, you could buy one share of Apple, but if the price of Apple goes up $1, what you've made is $1. To profit using shares of stock, say by swing trading, you need to own a lot of shares of stock. As we'll see in a minute price changes in the stock are magnified in the option. If Apple goes up $1, the options trader is going to be a lot better off than the guy who only buys one share with his $200.

Options Prices Change in Big Ways

The price or value of an option is directly related to the share price of the stock. It's not a one-to-one relationship in most cases, however. We'll see what the exact value is, but for now, let's say a call option for Apple stock is going to move in such a way that for every dollar Apple gains and loses, the price of the option will move by $0.80. This is on a per-share basis – so for the option overall, a $1 move in the stock means and $80 move in the value of the option.

This cut both ways, so options trading is not for the faint of heart. It also requires discipline. If you are watching an option over the course of a single day, you might see it go up and down by $50 in value if there is a lot of volatility.

But the advantage is a small price increase in a stock can lead to big profits very quickly. Suppose that you bought that Apple option for $125. If the price per share of Apple goes up $0.40, then the price of the option would rise to $157. Had it gone up $1, the option would rise in price to $205.

Remember that goes both ways, so a decline in price by 40 cents would drop a $125 option to $93. Option prices can move fast throughout the day, so you have to be keeping a close eye on it so you don't get wiped out and in order to take advantage of opportunities to sell for profits.

The amount that each option's price moves with respect to the price of the underlying stock is something that varies depending on the individual option. We will discuss how to figure out the possible price changes later.

Options Have a Higher ROI

The return on investment for an option is much higher than for stocks. Let's say you had $5,000 to invest, and we used that to buy Apple shares at $200 a share. That would give us 25 shares. So if the price went up by $2, that would give us a $50 profit, ignoring commissions. So we'd have an ROI of:

ROI = $50/$5,000 x 100 = 1%

That really isn't a bad share increase for a single day move, investors in stocks are looking for a return of maybe 8% *per year*.

We could buy 40 options contracts at $125 each. Using the previous example where a $1 move in the stock increases the per-share price of the option by $0.80 a $2 price increase would raise the price of the option from $125 to $285. The total profit per option contract is $160. Our net profit with $0 commissions on

Robinhood would be $6,400. The ROI in the options case is:

ROI = $6,400/$5,000 x 100 = 128%

There are even bigger opportunities than this, on certain days you'll see stocks make big moves, like after an earnings announcement. The share price could go up $10 or $20 if earnings beat expectations. The opportunities for profits are enormous.

Options are Flexible

It's common to talk about call options because the concept is easier for beginners to understand, But put options give the options trader advantages a stock investor doesn't have. What if instead, the stock price of Apple dropped $2? In that case, the investor in the Apple stock would lose $50 instead. It's not a huge loss to be sure, but a loss is a loss.

But a clever options trader who saw the decline coming could have bought put options with their money. For the sake of simplicity, assuming that the price of the option was the same and it related to the stock price in the same way, the price of the put options would go up by $6,400 when the price of Apple dropped $2.

And we'll see later that you can devise strategies that will earn profits no matter which way the stock price moves. These techniques go by the name of straddle, strangle, and iron condor among others.

Options are Fast

Options have an expiration date. Some people will see this as a negative, but others will find it refreshing. Since options have an expiration date, they are not assets that you're going to hold onto very long (except for LEAPS). For those that like an asset with an expiration date, the result of this on a practical level is that with options you are going to get in and get out of your trades pretty quickly. You might periodically do day trades when a stock is experiencing large price movements. I typically do 2-3 a week (remember don't do 4 a week, unless you plan to deposit $25,000 and accept the day trader designation). In most cases, you'll hold the option for a couple of days and then sell it when the opportunity arises. If you are selling to open, then you'll be holding the position for anywhere from a week to a month or two. But there is no long term investing.

Chapter 4: Buying and Selling Options

In this chapter, we are going to discuss basic options trading. Most readers are probably going to start off as level 2 options traders. This gives you the ability to buy to open a position. So you can buy options at what you hope is a low price, and then sell them at what you hope is a high price. Knowing when to buy and sell is something you have to learn from experience, but we can give you some general advice. You will also have to set up rules for cutting your losses.

Can you make profits buying call options?

The internet is full of nonsensical advice. The problem is that anyone can create a blog and write something that looks authoritative or they can make a YouTube video. Even some authoritative sites have articles that are clearly not written by someone who actually trades options. Many websites and YouTube videos are made by people that know what they are doing, but they are probably selling a training course or something and so you can take what they say with a grain of salt because they might have an agenda.

With that in mind, let's answer the basic question, can you profit buying call options?

The answer is obviously yes. But to do so, you have to do it carefully. The first step in doing this is to avoid letting "luck" determine your fate. You are going to need to choose when the right time is to get into an option. The second thing to keep in mind is the expiration date of the option. Third, to have a successful and profitable business buying options, you should set a pre-determined profit limit in order to take a fixed amount of profit.

Never Let an Option Run to Expiration

Options suffer from a problem called "time decay". The price of the option is the sum of two prices, the extrinsic price, and intrinsic price:

Option Price = Extrinsic Price + Intrinsic Price

The intrinsic price comes from the price of the underlying shares of stock. Depending on many different factors, it may be more or less influential on the total price of the option. Extrinsic value is "time value". So it's getting smaller as time passes. If the option is in the money, the intrinsic value can overwhelm the extrinsic value, but if the option is out of the money, then it's going to be all extrinsic value. In that case, the option can quickly dwindle to zero value as long as it stays out of the money. For that reason, you shouldn't hold on to an option hoping things will turn around. If you are hoping that the share price will turn around at some point but the option is a few days away from expiration, it's not worth holding onto. Cut your losses and buy another option with a further-out expiration date.

If you let your options run out to the expiration date, or even a couple of days before, you will end up losing all or a significant fraction of your money. Options that are out of the money 'expire worthless' on expiration day, so if you are still holding them, you lose all your money.

Set a Cutoff to Exit Your Trade

Before you start trading make rules that you are going to stick to. You could say, as an example, that you will sell an option if the price drops by $25. That gives it enough room in case the share price of the stock is going down but has enough momentum to turn around and rise again in price. If that doesn't happen, $25 is not a huge loss. So you can take the loss and move on. A trader has to be realistic and traders are not going to win on all trades. Selling at a $25 loss is better than losing your entire investment. Be sure to keep things in perspective, a $25 loss would be something you'd apply for an option that costs $100 or more, for smaller price options pick smaller values.

Pay Attention

You will have to pay close attention to the markets. So you will need to closely watch the charts to see if your exit cutoff is reached.

Become familiar with limit orders and use them

One way to protect yourself is to enter a limit order. A limit order is an order you place to buy or sell a financial security at a fixed price. When selling your option, it's a price you are willing to accept for the option. If you are trying to get out of an option because the price is strongly declining, then you should use a limit order so that you can get out of the option quickly before you lose most of your investment. Submit a price that matches the low end of the range when you need to get out.

Follow Trends

If you are buying call options, the best ones to look for are for stocks that are entering a trend. This isn't a book on technical analysis, but if you are interested you should look that up and study it. Generally, all you need to find out what the stock is going to do is use candlestick charts with a 9-period and 20-period moving average on the chart. You can learn about candlesticks and their meaning in order to anticipate what happens next. To buy a call option, you're going to want to buy the option when the stock is at the bottom of a downward trend, with signs of a trend reversal. You can learn to spot a possible trend reversal by learning about candles on stock charts. Also, you can look for crossovers between the moving averages. When the 9-period moving average crosses above the 20-period moving average, that is a good time to buy an option. Then you can ride the wave high enough until you earn enough profit. For me, if I am watching and see an option has earned $50 profit, I sell it and take my winnings. Sure sometimes I am going to miss out on profits, but that is life. The successful trader profits on most of their trades and isn't looking for a "big win".

If you are observant, you will be watching various stock charts and can spot a major trend. In these cases, you want to follow the trend. Remember it can be up or down. If the trend is down, buy a put option.

Following a trend can be a good way to earn a quick profit. Just be ready to exit the trend at the right time. That is something you will have to learn how to do with any level of precision. In order to gain the types of skills you need you should buy some books on technical analysis or watch YouTube videos about the topic. Make sure that you're watching videos about stocks and not the foreign exchange market although they both use some overlapping ideas.

Buying Multiple Contracts

So the profit level I am suggesting of $50 would be the profit per option contract. When you're first starting out you probably want to start you probably want to just trade one option contract at a time. But as you gain experience you are probably going to want to buy and sell multiples of the same option in order to magnify your winnings. Of course, you have to keep in mind that will magnify your losses as well, but it does make sense to buy five contracts of an option and make a profit of $250 then it does to just earn $50 if you know what you're doing and you have the capital to enter the positions. However, you need to be aware there may be certain issues that arise if you buy multiples of one option at the same time. The day trading limitations are always hiding in the background. You'll be able to buy the 10 options or 5 five options whichever you choose, but you might have to wait until the following day in order to sell them all. That kind of limitation might interfere a little bit with your trading. Of course, you can buy options of different strike prices for the same strike price in different expiration dates and avoid these kinds of problems. Remember that if options differ in some way, either with a different strike price or expiration date then they are not considered to be independent financial securities even though they control the same underlying stock.

How many different stocks?

New traders are understandably excited about getting into trading options. Asked such you might have the impulse toward wanting to buy options on all kinds of different stocks at the same time. So for example, you could buy an option on Netflix, an option on Google, an option on Facebook, and an option on Tesla. And maybe you would buy a few more too if you had the money.

That's a bad idea, however. The reason is you need to keep a close eye on your trades. If you buy options on six different stocks at the same time, you are going to be spreading yourself too thin. I recommend that people only enter positions on one or two different stocks at the same time. That doesn't mean you can't buy multiple options for each of the stocks, but instead of buying 10 options for 10 different stocks, you could buy six options on Tesla, and for options on Apple.

This is important to do so that you can follow the stock charts and price movements of the underlying stock and be ready to exit your positions on the moment's notice. That doesn't mean you have to be sitting in front of the computer full-time like some kind of DayTrade, but you do have to have an awareness and the ability to act fairly quickly. This is going to be really important if your options are not working out the way you   hoped.

The number of stocks, of course, will vary from person to person, but for most people following, to add time is a good number. Another factor here is of course how much time you can devote to your options trading. If you get to a point where are your options trading full-time then you may be able to pay attention to more than two stocks at once.

Picking Your Expiration Date

The expiration date is one of the most important things to keep your eye on when it comes to options trading. So question that many newbies have, and many experts like pontificating on, is how close to the expiration date should you buy the option? Most brokers aren't going to allow you to buy an option on the expiration date. And if you aren't planning to buy or sell the shares of stock you probably don't want to do that anyway. The day before the expiration date is also to close in order to enter any trades. So the first rule for buying options when it comes to the expiration date is don't buy them the day before expiration, or on the expiration date unless you hope to own the stock or sell it when the contract expires. If you don't exercise your rights on an expired option then you basically walk away with nothing.

Outside of that, the expiration date doesn't matter other than being aware of how the time decay of the option can affect the price of the option. If you hold options overnight, one of the things you're going to see early the next morning when trading begins is that you lose some money do the time decay. That money can be made back up if there is a significant movement in the price of the stock but you need to be aware that the time decay is going to be happening, and that it's really going to hurt you if the option price is not moving in your   favor.

One way to avoid this is to buy options that are far away from the expiration date. They hold a lot more time value than options that are close to the expiration date.

Let's be clear. You can definitely earn large profits on options that expire within a week or less. Remember that you don't want to buy an option on expiration day, and you don't want to buy an option the day prior to the expiration day. But I have purchased many options that expire in two days and I have been able to make significant profits from them. Options that are close to expiration can move very quickly in response to stock price changes. The only thing is you want to be sure that you can get out of an option before it's too late. So if you buy an option that expires two days away, plan on that being a day trade. You're not going to want to hold that option overnight. For one it might lose a lot of value the next day from the time decay and second, it might be hard to get rid of.

Buy Out of the Money or In the Money?

If you are looking to buy options as a straight trade, so in other words by a call option to make profits from an increase in share price, then one issue you need to consider is whether the option is in the money or out of the money. This is an area of importance to consider and many beginners actually mess this up.

There is a temptation to buy out of the money options because they are cheap. Let's take a look at some options for Apple that expire in a week. The share price is $202.96. And in the money call option which has a strike price of $202.50 is priced at $2.87 per share. So that means it would cost $287 dollars to buy it. A $207.05 strike price which is out of the money quite a bit, is only $0.81. In other words, it would cost $81. A $220 call is only priced at $0.03, so the total cost by it is only three dollars. That might seem like a good deal but the truth is it's a very bad deal indeed. That isn't going to go anywhere for you. Of course, you might make a little bit of money on it and if you lose out, it's only three dollars assuming that you only buy one. But that's just a dumb move to make.

So if you're going to buy call options in the hopes of making profits from rising stock prices, it's better to buy in the money options. There's more upfront investment but you're going to make a lot more money if your investment goes the right way. There is one alternative which I sometimes use and that is to buy options that are slightly out of the money. So if you are looking at Apple, in the share price is $202.50, it would be okay to try out of the money options up to about $205. When the share price is rising, those can gain quite a bit in revenue. On a popular stock or index fund it's also pretty easy to sell them off very quickly and so exiting your position will not be a problem.

Put Options

The same logic applies to put options, all you have to do is reverse the price relationships. So you are going to invest input options when you see signs of a declining price coming, or there is an obvious downtrend in the stock price. In this case, you just reverse all the relationships and so a slightly out of the money option is going to be one that has a strike price slightly lower than the share price. You'll be looking to profit from declining stock prices, and you'll look to exit your position when the share price is rising and it goes too high for acceptable losses.

A good trader is going to be versatile and be able to move back-and-forth between using put options and call options as the situation requires. That doesn't mean you can't just profit buying call options or vice versa, but you want to be able to earn profits at all times in the market. So if you've been playing a rising for a bullish market, in the market gets taken over by the bears then you should switch to using put options in order to earn money.

Basic Trading: Summary

In this chapter, we have addressed the simplest possible way that you can trade options and earn profits. That is by purchasing call options when you think the price of the stock is going to rise, and then selling a call option when the price reaches a take profit level that you have decided upon ahead of time. Of course, you should not just buy options when you think the prices going to rise. You should study technical analysis and candlestick charts and also listen to the financial news so that you know what's going on. You can never be certain which direction a stock is going to go on a particular day, or even over the course of a week. So all you can do is make an educated guess and be ready to exit the trades that don't work out for you.

So the first step toward success in using the strategy is to avoid randomly picking options to buy. Instead, you are going to use a methodical process and pick options for stocks where there is a reasonable belief based on evidence that the share price is likely to rise in the near future. In that case, you buy a call option. On the other hand, if your analysis shows that the stock is going to be declining in price, then you buy a put option. You should also be paying close attention to the price movements of the stock after you have entered a position. If you see a shift and it's pretty strong in the change of direction then you can always change your position by selling it and buying the opposite position.

Also, remember the need to set a criteria for exiting your positions. One that worked for me for a long time is to take $50 profits when they become available. And sometimes it will go higher and you can take a $65 or $100 dollar profit. But the point is to have some fixed acceptable level of profit to ensure that you can exit the position and earn money. Second, you should also have a criteria for getting out of the position when it's working against you. There aren't any specific rules to use for this. You can set your own, but the point is you should have the rules. The trader that doesn't have rules is going to end up floundering around, and the trader that has rules will end up profitable.

It's also advisable to keep a journal. I actually prefer doing this using a spreadsheet or you can even do it by hand in a notebook. You're not going to be doing any fancy calculations with it. The purpose of your journal is to record your trades and the profit and loss associated with each trade. You need to keep close track of it and really know whether or not you're earning profits from your activities. If you find that you're not earning profits, then you can try adjusting different parts of your strategy. You might be exiting your traits to early.

Something to consider is that stocks often drop in price, but they will often redound pretty quickly. So you don't necessarily want to sell your options at the first sign of trouble. The time you sell your options and possibly take a loss is when the signs are all pointing in that direction of a solid downtrend in price; or alternatively, if you are holding put options that would be an uptrend.

Chapter 5: Options Strategies Part 1

If you are a level II options trader, the only strategies that you can use are selling covered calls, selling protective puts, or buying calls and puts. Despite the way some people are dismissive of the possibility of making profits simply buying calls and puts, you can actually make significant profits using that trading method. But many traders are going to be interested in using more sophisticated strategies that can help them make profits and minimize losses no matter which direction the stock moves. And there are also strategies that can be used to make profits with unidirectional stock moves that hedge your potential losses. In this chapter, we are going to start taking a look at some of the options strategies that may be available to level 3 traders. The ones that we're going to talk about in this chapter our debit spreads, straddles, and strangles.

Assignment Risk

When you get into more advanced options trading strategies, you are going to have to worry about assignment risk. This is because many of the more advanced trading strategies are going to require you to sell an option as a part of the trade. Any time that you sell an option, if it goes in the money there is a chance that the option will be exercised. The risk here is that you are entering these strategies without backing them with shares of stock or money. If a buyer of an option decides to exercise the option, then we say that you (the seller) are assigned. Assignment means that you have to carry out the terms of the contract.

If an option expires in the money, it's going to be automatically exercised. It doesn't matter if the holder of the option wants to or not. The broker will do it.

The way to get around assignment is to exit the trade. If you sell an option, that means you buy it back when it gets close to expiration. You don't have to worry about the options that you have purchased. Any option that you buy carries no risk to you personally. The only options you have to worry about are those that you sell. So buy-back options that you sell prior to expiration. Because of time decay, you're going to still earn a profit buying it back.

It's important to know when an option might be exercised. Unless it's a European style option, it can be exercised on any date on or before the expiration date for the option. The criteria to be exercised is that the price of the shares must be higher than the strike price of a call, or they must be lower than the strike price of a put. Technically speaking, in those cases the options could be exercised. But they won't be exercised unless the price exceeds the break-even price of a call or falls below the break-even price of a put.

Let's say that you sell a call option with a strike price of $100. If the premium is $2, that means that the share price has to move above $102 for it to be worth it to the buyer to exercise the option. If the share price rises to $101.50, the option is in the money by $1.50. However, it's not worth it for the buyer to exercise the option, because they paid $2 to enter the position. They would have a net loss of $0.50 a share on that deal. So they won't exercise it until it goes above $102.

And the truth is that even then, depending on how much time value the option has, they still might not exercise it. That's because if they exercise the option they would eat the cost of the time value.

This works the same for a put option. So if you have a strike price of $50 and sell a put option for $1 a share, the price of the stock needs to fall below $49 for it to be worth it to the buyer to exercise the option.

So assignment is not a significant risk until the stock price moves beyond the strike price plus or minus the premium, or past the breakeven price. If there is a significant time until the expiration date, 3 days or more, assignment isn't likely in most cases. So don't panic if you sell an option that is a part of one of these strategies and the option goes in the money for a while.

When it gets close to the expiration date and you can close the position and make a profit, you simply buy back the option that you sold.

Debit Spreads

A debit spread is a method that is similar to buying a call or a put but in exchange for limiting the potential gains you can get from a trade, the probability of earning a profit is higher. The first debit spread that we are going to consider is called a call debit spread. The motivation for using a call debit spread is similar to buying a call option by itself. This is done in the belief that the share price of the stock is going to rise before the options expire.

With a called debit spread you buy and sell to call options at the same time. Depending on your broker you may have to be a level III options trader in order to execute this strategy. The reason is it involves selling an option. Second of all even though the option is being sold as part of a larger strategy, it's not going to be backed with anything and so could possibly cause some trouble which we will discuss later.

For call debit spread you have to call options and they will both have the same expiration date. However, they're going to have different strike prices. This mitigates your risk a little bit because by selling a call option you are going to receive a payment. A call debit spread is a debit, because you are going to purchase a more expensive call option with a lower strike price, and you're going to sell a lower-priced call option with a higher strike price. So the call option that you sell is going to partially offset the cost of the more expensive call option that you purchase.

The first thing to pay attention to what the debit spread is the breakeven price. For call debit spread, the breakeven price is the lower strike price plus the debit that was required to enter the position. So if you buy a call option with a $100 strike price that costs three dollars, and you sell a call option was $110 strike price for one dollar, first you calculate the difference between the premiums paid. So you've subtracted the premium for the higher strike price which is one dollar, from the premium you paid for the lower strike price which is $3. So that's $3-$1=$2. Then you add this to the lower strike price to get the breakeven. In this case that would be $100 +$2 =$102. That means the share price has to rise to $102 before you have a chance of seeing a profit on the deal. You will make money as long as the stock is in the range of the breakeven price up to the offer strike price. So in our example, as long as the share price ends up between $102 and $110, we can make a profit. If the price rises above $110, the gain is fixed but no longer increases. For a call debit spread, the possible profit is the difference in the strike prices minus the price paid to enter the position. In this example, the difference in the strike prices is $10, and the debit is $2, so the maximum profit is $8. That is on a per-share basis, so with 100 shares, it's $800.

To see the benefits of what the structure of the call debit spread can do here is an actual example of a Netflix debit spread. The lower strike price is $402.50. The cost to enter the position is $2.37. So the breakeven point is $404.87. Slightly above the break-even price, it would make a profit of a couple of hundred dollars. But the higher above the breakeven price, the higher the gain to a point. This one hits a gain of $2013 when it reaches the higher strike price of $425. If the price goes anything above that even $500 we won't see any more profits from the position.

To summarize, you enter a call debit spread when you think the share price is going to rise.

Put Debit Spread

A put debit spread works like a call debit spread, but it's used when you think the price of a stock is going down.

This works in a similar fashion, so you'll buy a put and sell a put with the same expiration date but with different strike prices.

In this case, with put options, you hope to earn profits from a declining share price and the option with the higher strike price. That is the option that you buy. You buy a cheaper put option that has a lower strike price to offset the cost and increase the probability of profits. The cost of entry for the position is the price of the higher strike option less the price you earn selling the lower strike price option.

The breakeven point is the difference in premiums, subtracted from the higher strike price. So if we buy a put option with a $100 strike price for $5 and sell a put option with a $90 strike price for $2, the difference in the premiums is $3, and the break-even price is $100 - $3 = $97.

The potential maximum profit is the difference in the strike prices minus the net premium, which for this case would be $100 - $90 - $3 = $7, times 100 shares gives a potential profit of $700.

A put debit spread, like a call debit spread, is a limited risk, but limited reward strategy to use with options, but in this case, you are hoping for a stock price decline. If the stock rises above the higher strike price, then you'll lose a fixed amount of money on the trade. The amount you can lose is given by the difference in premiums. For our example that is $3, for 100 shares the total loss potential is $300.

Strangle

A strangle is an options strategy that can be used when you think that the price of a stock is going to move a large amount, but you are not sure which direction the stock price is going to move. So a strangle is going to be profitable when the stock moves up, but it's also going to be profitable when the price of a stock moves down. A strangle is a good example of the power that options have when compared to trading stocks. A strangle involves buying a put and a call at the same time.

Strangles can be used at any time that you want to set up this kind of strategy. That way you don't have to worry about which direction the share price is going to move. The only thing with a strangle is that you are going to need the stock to move in a significant direction or another. So if the stock is ranging, that is stuck within a narrow range of prices and it's not moving one way or the other very much, then a strangle is not an appropriate strategy. But if you are seeing signs of or expecting a breakout, then a strangle can be a useful strategy.

A strangle is going to basically wipe out one of the options in the trade. If the share price goes up by a large amount, you are going to profit from the call option going in the money. The put option is going to expire worthless in that case.

On the other hand, if the share price drops by a very large amount, the put option will earn profit, but the call option will expire worthless.

A strangle uses the same expiration dates for both options, but they each have their own strike prices. The maximum loss is fixed but the maximum gain with a strangle is unlimited. Of course, it's not really unlimited because a share price is only going to go up so far, but the more the share price rises or falls the more your profits if the option that is bringing profits is in the money. On the upside, gains are theoretically unlimited because the share price could in theory rise to any value. On the downside, the potential profit is large but equal to the value that the stock would lose if it went to zero.

The premium paid to buy a strangle is used to calculate the break-even point. For the upper break-even point, that is important if the stock price goes up, the break-even is the premium + the upper strike price. For the lower break-even point, it's the strike price less the premium paid.

For an example, suppose that we entered a trade that required a $2.50 premium, with a strike price on the call at $110 and a strike price on the put set at $100. The break-even point on the upside is $110 + $2.50 = $112.50. The break-even on the downside is $100-$2.50 = $97.50. So if the stock is rising, it has to rise above $112.50 before we make profits. On the downside, it has to go below $97.50 before we make profits.

The maximum loss is limited to the premium paid to buy the call and put options. The loss will occur if the stock price stays in between the strike prices. So in this example, if the stock prices remain between $100 and $110, we would take the maximum loss on the trade. Most trading platforms allow you to enter into a strangle on a single trade, but you can buy them separately too and have the same situation for all practical purposes.

Strangles are an interesting way to extend your trading toolkit. They are easy to understand and easy to implement without requiring too much money, and there is no assignment risk. Note, however, that a strangle may carry a day trade warning and you might have to wait until the following trading day in order to sell it if for some reason you feel you want to get out of the position quickly.

If you are buying options hoping to see prices rise or fall, a strangle is a good addition to your overall strategy. That way you can see more profits when your bets don't necessarily go as planned.

The more narrow you make your strangle, the higher the odds of profit because there is a smaller range where the stock price would have to stay in order for there to be a loss incurred.

Straddle

A straddle is a bit similar to a strangle. In this case, you buy a call option and a put option at the same time. But with a straddle, you have a call option and the put option at exactly the same strike prices. The call and the put will have the same expiration date.

The purpose behind a straddle is the same as the purpose behind the strangle. That is, you use this strategy when you expect the stock Price to break one way or the other but you aren't sure if it's going to go higher or lower. Since the strike prices of the call and put in a straddle are the same, this means that the stock price doesn't have to move as much as it would for a strangle.

So let's say for example that we have a call option with the strike price of $100 and it cost one dollar to enter the position. If we were going to buy a strangle we might choose a put option with a strike price of say $96 dollars. But in the case of a straddle, you buy a put option with the same $100 dollars strike price. The breakeven point for a move to the downside is the strike price minus the cost to enter the position. So let's say for the sake of simplicity that the put option also cost one dollar. So the total cost to enter the position is $2. The breakeven price on the downside would be $100 -$2 = $98. The breakeven price on the upside is found by adding the total premium paid to the strike price. So this is going to be $100 + $2 = $102. If the stock remains within the range of the two breakeven prices, we are going to incur a loss. The maximum loss is equal to the premium paid. So, in this case, we paid $1 premium for each option, which means that the total loss is two dollars times 100 shares for a total loss of $200.

The theoretical maximum profit on the upside is unlimited. On the downside, it's equal to the price of the shares. So those are theoretical limits I guess it's possible that the price of the shares could go to $0, and sometimes that does happen but is extremely rare. So the profit is actually going to be the kind of profit you would earn from an in the money option, less the total premium paid. So let's say that the share price rose to $110. In that case, we would subtract the two dollars paid to enter the position. You would also subtract the strike price. The put option would expire worthless. So our profit would be $110 - $2 - $100 = $8, for 100 shares per the contract that would mean a total profit of $800. On the downside, if the price dropped to $90, we'd earn the same profit. This would be $100 - $90 - $2 = $8.

So like a strangle, a straddle represents a great opportunity to earn big profits when a stock is expected to make a big move.

Earnings calls

One of the biggest opportunities that you have as an options trader is to make big profits after earnings calls by large companies. After an earnings call, a stock can make a huge move in price. That might be permanent or not, but it's certainly going to hold for a time. The thing to look for in an earnings call is when the profits beat expectations. You will see news items that say something like a company reported earnings of $1.50 per share, beating analysts expectations of $1.30 a share. That seems like no big deal, but announcements like this can send the price of a share skyrocketing.

In the past, earnings calls by major companies like Facebook, Netflix, Google, and Apple have sent share prices up by $10-20 a share. Remember this can lead to massive gains when it comes to options. You want to get into your position a week or two before the earnings call so that you can profit from the big move.

Of course, the earnings call is just as likely to be a disappointment. If the earnings expectation was $1.30 a share, but they report actual earnings of $1.15 a share, that is going to send stocks dropping like a rock. So they might drop $10 - $20.

This is the beauty of the straddle and strangle strategies. Before an earnings call, nobody has any idea whether or not the stock is going to exceed or fail to meet the expectations. Whether or not this has any value in the real world isn't really relevant. A company may fail to meet expectations but still be profitable. But in the bizarre world that we live in it's the expectations that carry the weight. And so if a company is not living up to expectations, that means you can expect to see big   drops   in   the   share   price.

But if you put a strangle or straddle on the stock before the earnings call, you don't care which direction it moves. The only worry you're going to have is whether or not you chose your strike prices in such a way that you can ensure that the share price is going to exceed the breakeven point on the upper end, or fall below the breakeven point on the lower end. Given the history of earnings calls for the blue-chip companies and big tech companies, the chances are extremely high that your expectations   for   this   are   going   to   be   met.

One strangle or straddle has the potential to bring in a couple of thousand dollars in profit in a single day. Checking up a past Facebook's earnings call, the following day to share price jumped by $20. In order to get in the position, you might have to spend around $450. But when you consider hey rise of share price by twenty dollars, you could be looking at a profit of around $1500.

So when the situation calls for it a straddle or strangle is an excellent strategy to use. The only time it's never going to work is one of those periods when a stock is ranging in between narrow values and doesn't seem to be moving anywhere. So before you set up a straddle or strangle, be sure to study the recent behavior of the stock to make sure that is not stuck in some range at the present time.

Chapter 6: Options Strategies Part 2

In the last chapter, we examined some options strategies designed to keep our losses capped while increasing the probability of profit. The strategies still required us to end up buying options. In this chapter, for the first time, we are going to consider some strategies that are centered around selling options. You only have to have a level III designation in order to use them.

First, we are going to look at call credit spreads. This is also buying and selling a call just like we discussed in the last chapter. But this time it's going to be set up so that you get a credit to your account, rather than a debit. The option is going to have to go towards expiration in order to actually realize the credit. The purpose of a credit spread is going to be opposite to that used for debit spread. So while a call debit spread would be something you use when you expect the stock price to rise, a call credit spread is something you use when you expect the stock price to drop. The reasons that this is the case will become clear when we illustrate it with specifics.

In addition, your brokerage firm is going to require a certain amount of collateral in order to enter the positions. This will be collateral in the form of cash. However, it won't be the full amount of collateral that you would expect.

The second strategy we're going to look at is a put credit spread. So, in this case, we are again going to be buying and selling input at the same time in order to create a spread, but the spread, in this case, is going to given that credit to our account. A put credit spread is a strategy used when you think the stock price is going to rise. The idea is to

Finally, we are going to look at hey strategy called Iron condor. The iron Condor is an interesting strategy that can be used when you think the stock price is going to be confined between an upper and lower value. So the iron Condor is essentially an opposite position when compared to a straddle or strangle. That is, you would consider using an iron condor when you don't expect the price of the stock to move very much.

Put Credit Spread

A put credit spread is a strategy used when you expect the share price of a stock to go up. The purpose of a put credit spread is to earn income. You must be a level 3 trader in order to use a put credit spread. A key distinction to think about with a put credit spread is that you are selling it to open the position. So we are leaving the realm of buying options and entering a new type of trading where we are selling options to make money, in the form of income. If you know how to use these strategies correctly you can earn a regular income on a weekly basis.

Put Credit Spread

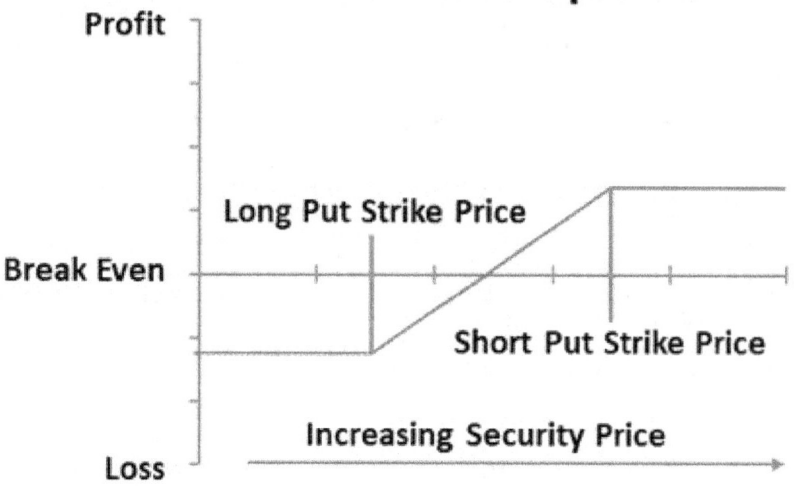

To set up a put credit spread, you choose a put that is out of the money but at a relatively high strike price, and you will sell this put option. Then you will select a put option that is further out of the money and buy it in order to reduce your overall risk.

The difference in the premiums is going to be your profit. So, if the first put option has a strike price of $100 and you get a $1 premium from it, and you select a $90 put option with a $0.40 premium to sell, then the difference in premiums is $1-$0.40 = $0.60. That is the net credit to your account, times one hundred shares you'd get $60 for this particular credit spread.

The danger with a put credit spread is the risk of assignment. Please see our discussion in the previous chapter for the details, but you're going to want to keep your eye on the price if it drops close to the higher strike price for the put options. The strike price minus the premium earned is the breakeven point at which someone might exercise the option. But generally speaking, unless it goes way in the money you don't have to worry about assignment unless it's near expiration.

One risk of assignment we didn't talk about is the last trading day. On the last trading day, although it's unlikely that the stock is going to make a sudden and dramatic move, there is that possibility. So you don't want to change it by holding the option on the last trading day even though academic treatments of this topic talk about the options expiring worthless while you walk away with your premium. If the stock did make a big move on the expiration day, you risk assignment when the option expires if it goes in the money. That would mean you would have to sell 100 shares of the stock to the buyer at the strike price.

In order to minimize risk and avoid these kinds of situations, a big part of the strategy is to buy back the spread. Your broker will have a "close" button in its interface for your credit spread, and you can buy it back by clicking on the close button to "close the position".

So you aren't going to make maximum profit, but by the time the options are about to expire worthless, you won't have to spend much to buy it back. Using our example, if we sold it for $60, you could buy it back for say $10 and make a $50 profit. It's not worth risking going into assignment for the extra $10.

Time Frames

There is some disagreement on what time frames, that is days to expiration that you should use when selling options. Many experts advise selling 45 to 30 days from expiration. This can be advantageous as you earn a premium from the decaying time value of the option, on the other hand, you are taking more risk that the stock is going to be able to move outside the boundary that you have set for it, and then you might be facing assignment risk. Remember, however, that anyone who buys the option risks losing because of the time value as well.

Others have suggested selling options on a weekly basis. Some even sell the day before or on the expiration day. The premiums collected are going to be smaller, but on the other hand, you get a low-risk quick sale (that is provided that you actually find a buyer). This strategy might work with options that have very high volumes. For example, you could use this on the ETF SPY.

Sell Out of the Money for Low Risk

One strategy that many professionals use is selling far out of the money options. This lowers their risk because there isn't much chance that the option is going to be exercised. You can do this far from expiration or close to expiration, but either way, you're going to have to sell many options in order to make a living. As an example, we could sell a put credit spread on SPY that expires in 2 days. The share price is $299, so I could pick a $292 put to sell at $9, and buy a $289 put for $5, for a net profit per contract of $4. The problem with this strategy is that at $4 per sale, you'd have to sell a huge number of them to make any kind of profit.

There will also be a large collateral requirement. When you are selling spreads, you don't have to put the collateral up in order to cover the actual purchase of shares, but you have to cover the loss that in theory could occur. For one of those spreads making $4, you need to cover it with $188. That isn't a very good deal.

So let's consider what happens when you look further out. Going about 30 days to expiration, we are going to find that the premiums for each option are quite a bit higher. A $295 put is selling for $3.05, so we could earn $305 from it. However, even though this is SPY, it might be hard to sell. The volume is only 8 and the open interest is 4. But we could buy the $290 put for $2.02 to close the deal. That's a net credit per share of $1.04, so we could earn $104 from the contract. You'd have to put up $288 in collateral.

To sell 100 contracts, which in this case may not be possible because there is tiny open interest for the option we are selling, we'd have to deposit about $39,000 into our account, but we'd earn $10,000 as long as the stock price didn't drop below the strike price of the option we're selling.

That sounds like a lot, but can you think of any other way to generate $10,000 of income from $39,000? If you put that in stocks you'd make $5,000 a year or so in a bull market. In the bank these days you'd make a few hundred dollars. So this is a really good way to generate income – if you can find buyers for your options. It's an astounding rate of return on your money.

If you go closer to the money, then you will have a higher chance of selling your spread, but there is also going to be a higher risk that at some point it's going to be assigned. Let's take an example using an almost at the money put that expires in two weeks. We can sell a $297 put for $2.67, and buy a $293 put for $1.68. The net credit is $0.99 a share, or $99 in total. To do this deal we'd need $192 per contract in collateral to cover possible losses.

To reduce the collateral required, you close the distance in between the strike prices. So if instead of $297/$293 we used $297/294, we'd need $112 in collateral per contract but we'd also reduce the credit to our account, this time we'd only earn $79.

What happens if the price heads south?

Let's say that the stock price drops by a lot, exceeding the strike price of the option that you purchased and it expires. In that case, the brokerage will exercise the option you bought, and then assign you the shares for the higher strike price that you sold. Using the last example, if the share priced dropped to $290, then the brokerage would sell 100 shares for us at $293 a share (remember that it's a put option). Then you'd have to buy 100 shares at $297 a share for assignment on the option with the higher strike price. So our loss would be the difference between the two deals, which is $4 a share for a total loss of $400.

Of course, the way to avoid these situations is to buy the spread back and close your position before things look too bad. Remember that when the share price is in between your two strikes, you're not protected by the lower strike put option, so you still risk assignment.

Call Credit Spread

Next, we are going to talk about the call credit spread. You would use this type of strategy when you think that the share price is going to drop. The central idea is to get your call options to expire worthless by choosing out of the money strike prices.

To create a call credit spread we start off by purchasing a call option that is a little bit out of the money and so although it's out of the money we can collect a healthy premium for it. We simultaneously sell a call option that is even further out of the money and we receive some protection from buying that option.

In this case, if the share price works rise above the lower call strike as long it was above the break-even point, there would be a risk of assignment if it was still below the outside call. Assignment, in this case, would require us to sell shares at a straight price. Chances are if you are using the strategy you don't own any shares. So the one thing we want to avoid is having the Share price exceed the lower strike price of the call option. In the event that the share price goes above the higher call option, we are in a similar situation will develop that we saw in the case of the put credit spread.

So, in this case, let's save it for the sake of an example we sell a call option with a $100 strike price. Then we buy a call option with a $103 strike price. In the event that the share price rose above $103, we would be assigned in the case of the $100 strike price. The brokerage would handle this for us so we don't have to actually buy the shares. So the shares would be sold at $100 a share. Then the brokerage would exercise the higher strike price option on our behalf. So they would get the shares at $103 and then sell them on the market. So now we have a difference in the strike prices which is three dollars, and that would be our total loss.

So once again the danger zone is if the share price ends up in between the strike price is at expiration. In that case, were not covered by the outside strike price. So we will be for then the brokerage would exercise the higher strike price option on our behalf. So they would get the shares at $103 and then sell them on the market. So now we have a difference in the strike prices which is three dollars, and that would be our total loss.

So once again the danger zone is if the share price ends up in between the strike prices and expiration. In that case, were not covered by the outside strike price. That means we would face risk of assignment for the $100 call. The key here is to avoid going into assignment in the first place. So just like with the other ones the same strategy applies with the car credit spread. All we have to do is close our position before the option expires, and the procedure for doing this is to buy it back. Time decay will have worked in our favor, and so chances are we can buy it back and earn a substantial profit from the difference of the original credit and the price paid to buy it back.

Like a put credit spread a call credit spread can be a good way to earn regular income using options.

Iron Condor

Let's review what we did in the last two sections. First, we considered a put credit spread which is a strategy that you would use when you were considering a stock that should go up in price. As long as it stays above the higher strike price, we can earn a profit on the deal. After we talked about the put credit spread, we considered Hey call credit spread which is used for the opposite situation. That is what I call credit spread your hoping that the stock price is going to drop. Specifically, you're hoping it's going to stay below the strike price used for the call option that you sell.

✕

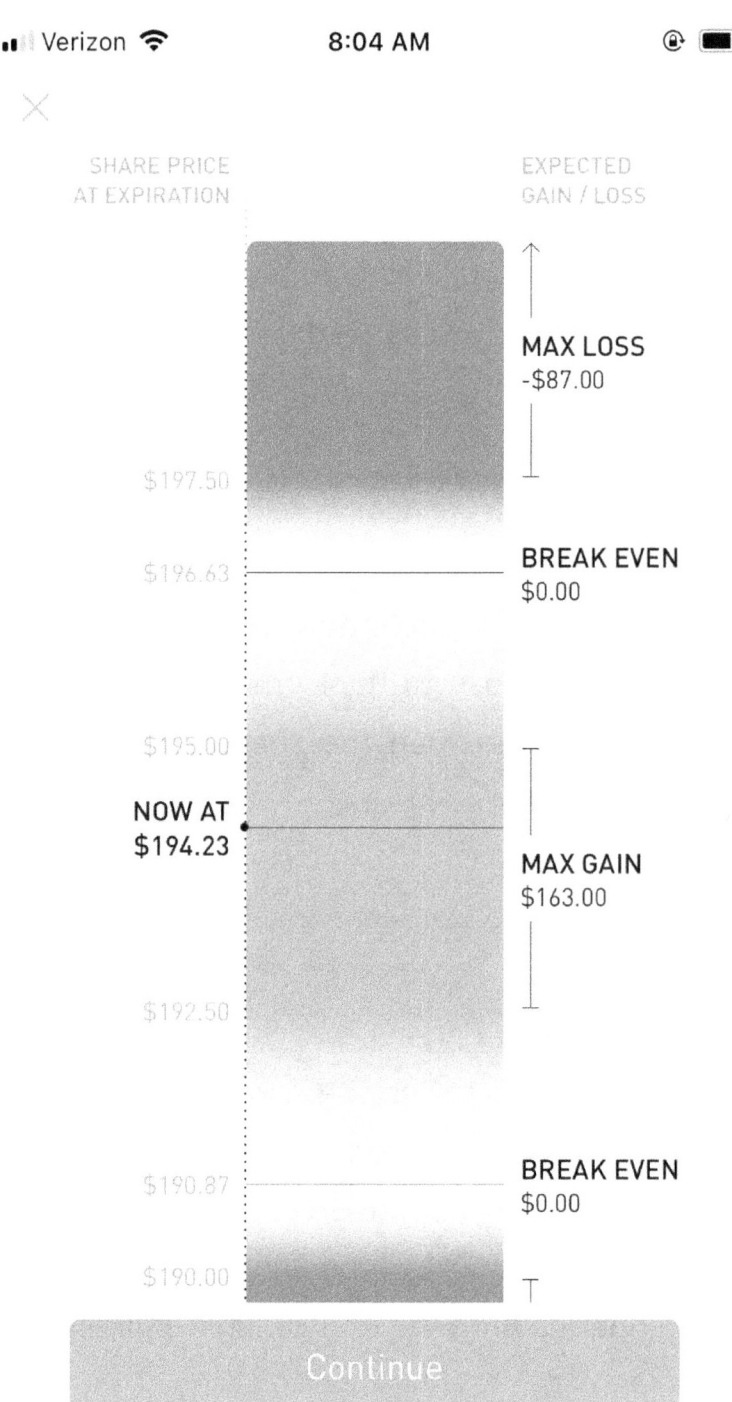

SHARE PRICE
AT EXPIRATION

EXPECTED
GAIN / LOSS

MAX LOSS
-$87.00

$197.50

$196.63   BREAK EVEN
$0.00

$195.00

NOW AT
$194.23   MAX GAIN
$163.00

$192.50

$190.87   BREAK EVEN
$0.00

$190.00

Continue

So what would happen if we combine these two strategies into a single strategy? In that case, we would get the iron condor. An iron condor is a concept that intimidates a lot of people who are new to options, but all it is a combination of a call credit spread, and a call put spread.

So if one part of the iron condor is used to earn profits when the share price drops, and the other part of the iron condor is used to earn profits when the share price rises, then it makes sense to think that an iron condor is going to earn profits when the share price actually stays in between the strike prices.

That is exactly what the iron condor does. The purpose of an iron condor is to trap the stock price within two boundaries. So the two options that you sell as part of the deal which is going to include a put option with a lower strike price, and a call option with a higher strike price, set boundaries for the stock price. In other words, what you want is for the stock price to stay within the boundaries until the iron condor expires.

Then using the same principles outlined when we discussed credit spreads, we are going to buy a call option with a higher strike price, and buy a put option with a higher strike price, in order to mitigate possible losses. The same principles discussed as far as assignments and exercise in the options when we talked about the credit spreads apply here. Unfortunately having to buy two options will cut Into our total profit, but it does give us some protection.

In order to use an iron condor, you must be a level III trader. A single iron condor is not going to typically bring a huge amount of profit. So if you are planning to use iron condors as an income strategy, plan on setting up a lot of them. They also require collateral. Typically for one at a time, it's not going to be very much money. And just like our examples in the previous section even when you're required to put in significant collateral in order to get an income of say $10,000 a month, compared to any use of money this is one of the best ways by far.

The possible loss isn't necessarily going to be the same on both sides of the iron condor. For example, a recent

Facebook iron condor has a possible loss on the downside of $91, while the possible loss on the upside is $191. The amount of collateral required for an iron condor is going to be equal to the maximum possible loss. So in the case of this Facebook iron condor, that is going to be $191.

However, the income earned from the iron condor is going to be $290. That seems like a fair trade. So you are getting paid $290 with a possible loss of $191 of the stock most of the upside and $91 if it moves to the downside. Note that these values are unique to this particular iron condor. It will depend on how it's set up as far as how the losses are distributed. In other words, sometimes there will be equal losses on the upside and downside, or there may be a situation where the losses on the upside are smaller than the potential losses on the downside.

It's important to get clear that with an iron condor this is another strategy that you sell in order to open the position. So you don't buy an iron condor even though some people argue over the semantics. You sell the iron condor because it's the inner strikes which are sold that are important.

So what are you have to have is collateral in order to cover potential losses, you are going to get a credit to your account when the iron condor expires. Alternatively, if you think there is a risk of it going in the money either on the upside or downside, you can buy it back before that happens. Again because of time decay, you are going to be able to buy it back at a cheap price relative to what you paid for it. Therefore you're still going to own a profit.

So if you're looking to make money from options as an income basis, an iron condor is definitely something that can be used as a part of your strategy.

Sometimes iron condors won't have risk on both sides. By choosing a far out of the money iron condor you can set up a situation where you make a smaller gain but there is no upside risk. Consider an iron condor on SPY. In this case, we have a big spread with a $271 strike price for the put that we sell and a $321 straight price for the call that we sell. There is almost a virtual certainty that it's going to stay within these ranges at least in the near term. There would have to be a major rally for it to go from where it is now which is about $299 over $321. I'm not saying that's not possible, but what I am saying is that the probability is working in your favor. So, in this case, the maximum gain happens when the share price is above $271 and below $321. In this case, the gain is $151. If the share price actually goes above the upper strike price they're still gain but it's reduced. In that case, you only have a gain of $51. The trade-off for this type of set up is that the maximum loss is going to be higher. For this particular example, it's $849. So for this to work we'd have to tie up $849, in order to make probably $151. That doesn't sound as appealing as the other one but at the same time, there simply isn't any other way to have money or make money the way that options can using the strategies.

And keep in mind if you're worried about losses to the downside, you can always buy the iron condor back before it expires. That way you won't be saddled with the possible risk of assignment.

Summary

In this chapter, we've learned about several successful strategies that can be used in order to generate monthly income for your account. As a trader, it's not an either-or situation. So you can create a mix of different approaches, using different strategies when appropriate. Before deciding which strategies, you are going to use, you should determine what your goals are. Is your goal to make massive profits? Are you looking to lower risk while generating income?

If you are looking for massive profits, then you might want to stick to buying options and trading them for profit, with the occasional strangle and straddle. If you are looking to minimize risk and generate income, iron condors might be more suitable. Of course, it's not always a black and white issue. You can do a mixture of both if you are able to wrap your mind around it. Some beginners have problems trying to keep track of everything and that can be a problem, but once you've gained experience buying and trading, it will be easier to start selling iron condors.

Chapter 7: Selling Options as a Strategy

In this chapter, we are going to turn our attention in a new direction. Actually, it's more of an evolution since we were discussing protected ways to sell options when you don't have actual control of any stock. We're going to start off in this chapter by considering the case where you *do* have control of the stock and how you can use that to generate income by selling options against it. Then we'll talk about using cash in your account in order to sell put options.

Next, we are going to talk about *selling naked*. This is not some kind of rude comment, what it actually means is selling options with nothing to back them. This is how the situation is framed, but the reality is you do have to have something to back the options. It's just that the requirements are greatly reduced. Brokerages have a rule that is used to calculate the required collateral in order to sell a naked option. You can look up the formula for your brokerage.

Although it will require you to put up some money, it's going to be far less money than you would have to put up otherwise. For a protected put you have to actually cover the price of the shares of stock. So, suppose we were looking at something like Apple. We could be talking about $20,000 in order to sell one contract.

If you sell naked, while you do have to put up some collateral, it's going to be a much smaller amount in comparison. I haven't done the calculation and don't have a specific option in mind (which you need to have in order to do the calculation), but it's going to be a couple of thousand dollars.

There are different ways that you can make money, by choosing different strike prices and expiration dates. Some traders are cautious and so they prefer to work far out of the money. Remember that this is all a probability game. The issue at hand is really - what is the probability that the option is going to expire in the money?

You can get an estimate of that from a quantity called *Delta* that can be looked up for any option. So, if Delta is 0.46, that means there's a 46% chance that the option will expire in the money. If Delta is 0.22, that means there's only a 22% chance that the option will expire in the money.

Of course, you have got to remember that this is *all probability* - and most of the time these strategies are going to work, as long as you avoid obvious times when a stock price can really move like an earnings call or dividend payment. But there are going to be some times when there are freak situations and something with the small Delta actually does expire in the money.

Covered calls

The first selling strategy that we're going to look at is known as a *covered call*. In order to sell a covered call, you must own 100 shares of the underlying stock. So, if you have 100 shares of IBM stock, you can sell call options against the stock every month and earn money on it.

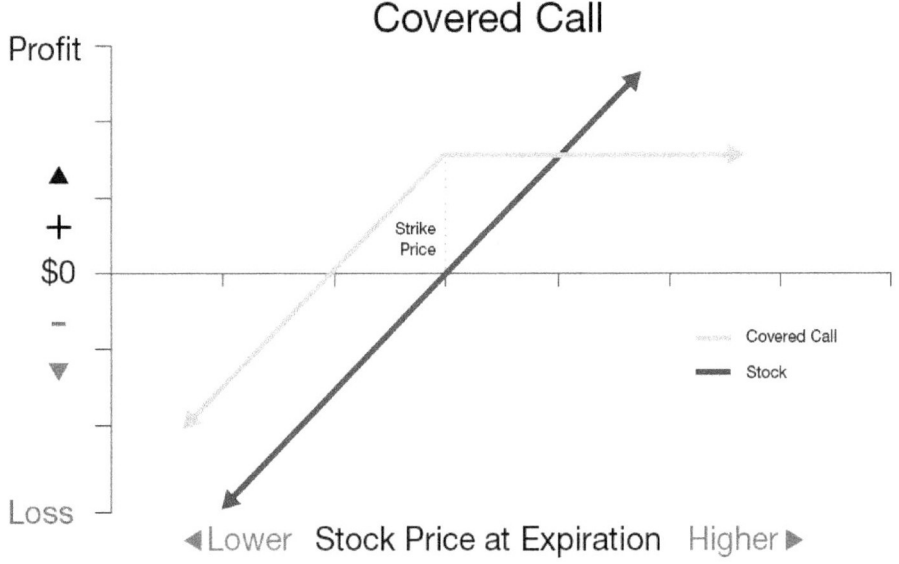

Covered Call

Profit

▲
+
$0
–
▼

Loss

Strike Price

Covered Call
Stock

◀Lower Stock Price at Expiration Higher▶

The smart way to do this is to sell options are out of the money, but that means that you're going to receive a smaller premium for it. Let's take a look at IBM for a specific example. The share price is $141.19. Most of the time IBM doesn't move around that much, it's kind of a slow-moving stock. A $145 call is selling for $2.85. So, you could sell one of those and earn $285 a month. Or consider a $150 call which has a much lower risk since it's further out of the money, it sells for $1.12, and so you could earn $112 a month from that one.

Something to remember is that you can only sell one call per 100 shares. So if you own 100 shares of IBM and you sell a call, that means you won't be able to sell another one until that option expires. If you were a smart investor and you racked up 10,000 shares of stock over time, then you would be able to sell a large number of call options on your stock.

That means if you have a large number of shares, you could earn a very substantial income. You could hold 5000 shares a reserve in reserve and sell call options on the rest. That would give you an income of $14,000 a month. So if you have a substantial portfolio of stocks it's possible to use this strategy in order to generate monthly income.

In practice, you would probably use different strike prices that would help spread out the risk. Although the risk is small, there is always a chance that at some point the share price is going to exceed the strike price of one of your call options, and it's going to get exercised. So in that case, while it wouldn't be catastrophic, it would probably be undesirable. You would have to sell your 100 shares.

Of course, the same strategy for protection could always be used here which would be to buy back any options that you sold in order to avoid assignment. But hopefully, a person using the strategy would be doing so in a smart way so that they wouldn't have to worry about assignment in the first place. The smart way to do it is to sell out of the money options.

Protected Put

This is a little bit different so let's remember how a put option works. In the case of a put option, we are looking for a share price to drop. Of course, the person selling a put option is hoping that the share price isn't going to drop low enough to be relevant to their option. But if it does drop that much, the buyer of the option has the right to sell shares at the strike price. So let's say that this share price drops from $90 a share to $50 a share, and the strike price is $80. So the owner of the put option can buy 100 shares at $50 a share. Then they can exercise the option and sell the shares at the strike price of $80. That would give them a profit of $30 per share.

So that's a review of what a put option is in case you weren't sure. So let's talk about selling a *protected* put.

When you sell a put option, you are banking on the share price staying high. So selling a put option is a bullish move. Buying a put option is a bearish move.

Selling a put option is quite a risk if it ends up getting exercised. So you have to be able to buy the shares if they are "put" to you. That can amount to a large amount of money. For this reason, brokerages aren't all that anxious to let people sell put options.

To sell a protected put, you have to put the cash that would be required in the event the option was exercised to purchase the shares. So if the strike price is $50, you need to have 100 x $50 = $5,000 in your account to cover the put option. That way if it's exercised, you'll be able to do it and not get the broker in trouble. In exchange for this, you might make $100 selling the put.

But there is a lot you can do with $5,000, so I am not sure why anyone would bother tying up all their capital to make such a small amount of income. You may as well put it in the bank for that small amount of money, at least you won't be at risk of having to buy 100 shares of stock.

Put Options as Insurance

Some readers may be wondering why you have put options aside from gambling. The real reason that put options exist is to provide insurance. That is, the seller of a put option is assuming the risk with a stock. Many big players buy put options to insure their stock against catastrophic losses. So if you buy a put option with a strike price of $50, that limits any possible risk you have in holding the stock so that you don't end up losing that extra $50 a share if the stock went to zero. The seller of the put option is agreeing to buy the shares at $50, so if the stock price really did drop to $0, then the seller of the put option has taken on the risk and absorbed the loss for the other party. That is why when you sell put options people say that you are selling "premium". This is insurance premiums.

Selling a protected put option is a waste of your money. If you had the large amount of capital that is required to sell a protected put option, you'd be tying up a lot of money in order to make a couple of hundred dollars.

Selling Naked Puts

Selling naked put options is one of the most popular ways to earn an income from options. In this strategy, you don't have to keep all the money that would be required to cover the sale of stock at the strike price in your account. Instead, the first thing you do is open a margin account.

Remember, a margin account is an account that can be used to borrow money from a broker. In this case, brokerages will have a formula that they use to determine the amount of money that you need to have in your account. It's going to depend on the strike price of the option, the current share price, and a few other factors. Each brokerage may do it a little bit differently. So you should check with your brokerage to see what the specific rule is.

The amount of cash required is going to be much smaller than what would be required for a protected put, but you are probably still going to have a couple of thousand dollars up to maybe $10,000 in order to make a living doing this.

So the first part of the strategy that many people take is that you are going to sell put options that are far out of the money. You want to minimize the probability that they are going to be exercised. So for example, if you sell a put contract that has a delta of 0.22, that means there is only a 22% chance of the option going in the money by expiration. So worrying about assignment is moot.

In each individual case, you would have to check the volume and open interest to determine whether or not it's worth selling a particular option. But in this strategy, there is no *buying* on your part going on. If you follow the strategy all you were doing is selling option premium. This is important to emphasize because for beginners the idea of being involved in the stock market without buying something is a new way to think of things.

Many big successful traders do nothing but sell put options. You can easily make $1 million a year doing it. Some of the advice used in the other sections applies here as well. So you don't want to be concentrating on too many companies because you need to be well informed about what's going on. Among other things, each week you need to assess your risk of being assigned. That means carefully tracking the share price of each stock. As we advised earlier, you simply don't want your attention spread too thin.

We also have to consider the expiration dates of the options that we sell because if we go out 30 to 45 days, rather than selling options that are going to expire quickly, we can earn a lot more premium from the sale. Of course, this is assuming that the options are going to expire out of the money. But if everything is chosen carefully, there is a good probability that things are going to work in your favor. You can expect that to happen around 70% of the time.

There are some traders that do things differently, however. This is actually going to sound familiar because we discussed a similar issue in the last chapter. So in this case what you can do is you can sell options that expire within a week or less. The trade-off with this strategy is that you're going to get paid a smaller premium. But if the option is out of the money, over a week it doesn't have very long left to live. What that means is there's going to be massive time decay and that brings us to the possibility of the option expiring worthless. Or you could buy it back the day before expiration for pennies on the dollar. And this happens really fast over the course of one week. So each week you would set up enough options to make whatever income you had in mind, and sell them off. Hopefully, they would sell quickly because with the week you don't have much time to mess around.

From here, it's a matter of just watching the options to make sure there isn't any chance that they end up in the money.

Selling naked put options is one of the most popular methods used by experienced options traders. It's pretty low risk and it brings a regular income. You can easily make a million dollars a year from it if you build up over time. The only requirement is you are going to have to set up a margin account which means depositing $2,000 at least. To get an idea of what is required, to make $2,000 a week using tasty works selling certain put options, I'd have to deposit $11,000. That would be a pretty good tradeoff, you are just holding the $11,000 in the account and each week you sell $2,000 worth of options, and now you have an annual income of around $104,000.

Selling Naked Call Options

Since we've been talking about selling put options, it's not going to be a surprise that the next strategy is to sell naked call options. But this exposes the beauty of options once again. While everyone else is panicking trying to figure out whether the stock market is going up or down, as an options trader it really doesn't matter. To clarify this, I will tell you that selling naked put options is a strategy that is used in a bull market. Since stock prices are rising, it makes sense to sell options that are unlikely to be exercised because the stock price is never going to drop down that far.

Conversely, suppose the market is in a downturn. That would make selling put options less appealing and possibly raise the risk of doing so. This is where call options come to our rescue. If it was 2008 and the stock market was tanking, rather than being part of the frenzied sell-off, you could be selling call options.

And there's really no worry, after all, look at all the people who are buying put options now that are far out of the money, even though the stock market is on a rising path that never seems to end. So if the market was going the other direction you would find people, who for whatever reason that only they know, would be willing to buy call options under those circumstances.

So as an options trader, you have to be flexible. And that means being ready to move in between selling call options and put options as the situation demands. Of course, you could apply the other strategies that we discussed earlier, so, for example, you can sell call credit spreads when the market is in a downturn.

Selling a naked call is virtually identical to selling a naked put as far as the basic ideas. But in this case, we are hoping that the share price doesn't rise above our strike price. You'll also have to have some level of collateral in your account similar to the case with the naked put option. The principles other than that would be basically the same. So if you're in a bear market you would be selling out of the money call options and pocketing the income every week. Then when the market hit bottom and started reversing ending the recession, then you would change your approach and return to selling naked put options.

Chapter 8: Avoiding Beginner Mistakes and Tips

In this chapter, we are going to gather together all our best tips and advice for avoiding common beginner mistakes. It's very easy for beginners to make mistakes when trading because it's exciting and stressful all at the same time. Let's take a look at some of the mistake's beginners are prone to and think about how to avoid them.

Panicking and exiting early

In the early chapters of the book, I did emphasize that you should have a criteria for exiting a position that isn't going in your direction. However, you need to have some flexibility because small moves in the stock translate into big moves in an option. So you might see your option show up at some $40 in the red. That is an unpleasant prospect but that means that the stock might Have dropped by something like $.60. Now if you think about that you know that it's not uncommon at all for a stock to drop 60 or $.70, and then rebound in the upper direction by a dollar. So to sell off your option just because there is a small dip like that--unless it's clear that it's part of the downward trend--would be a foolish move. Know that if you think about that, it's not uncommon at all for a stock to drop 60 or $.70, and then rebound in the upper direction by a dollar. So to sell off your option just because there is a small dip like that unless it's clear that it's part of the downward trend, would be a foolish move. But we can forgive beginners for making a mistake of that nature. It's easy to get panicky when you start seeing your money slip away right before your own eyes.

To deal with these types of situations it's really important to understand a little bit about technical analysis and candlestick charts. These topics are beyond the scope of this book, but you can find information about these topics online, on YouTube, and of course in many books. The point of learning these tools is so that you can look at the chart and estimate where the stock is heading. The tools are far from perfect otherwise everyone would be multimillionaires. However, they are pretty good at giving you an idea that I would call an educated guess. It's better to make an educated guess then it is to panic and sell your option. When I first started, I made the mistake of exiting positions far too early and I would look back later and find that if I had stayed in I would've made a massive profit. Remember the stock market is always fluctuating a great deal.

Getting Involved in Many Trades at Once

As we've said multiple times spreading yourself too thin is a really bad idea when it comes to trading. The matter what strategy you decide to adopt, my belief is that you should focus on a few different securities and no more. so what you might sit down and do is pick five stocks that you were really interested in. Hopefully, these are big companies because you want liquidity in the options. Another thing you want is a relatively high share price so that the options have a chance to profit. Know if you are selling options or credit spreads, you definitely want a high share price so that you can earn from the premium. Once you pick out your five companies you should study everything about the companies and know them inside and out. That means looking at their financial statements, knowing when their earnings calls are, and keeping track of things like the volatility, and price to earnings ratio. Then you should study the charts of that company for the past 12 months. Familiarize yourself with the range is that the price has gone through over the past year. None of this is full proof but you were going to be far better off if you were informed rather than simply winging it when trading options.

So what happens if you do more than five companies? At some point, you're going to be spreading yourself too thin. If you trade more than five at once it's going to be hard to keep track of the changes in the share prices of companies that you are trading. And to decide whether to get in or out of trades you need to be keeping a close eye on everything. Now some people are maniacs and they are able to divide your attention very well and they like high pressure. If you are a so-called type a personality that likes high pressure then maybe you can go with as many as you want. But my advice for beginners is that you were going to be better off focusing on a smaller number of companies that you can really study and pay attention to.

Using Too Many Strategies

As I said before one of the first things you should do is sit down and figure out what your goal is with trading options. You don't want to be using a haphazard approach and trying to do this and that and seeing what happens. Instead, decide what your goal is in the best way you want to achieve that goal. Then look at all the different strategies that are available and see what is

The most compatible with your goals. Then apply maybe two or three different strategies at a time. There has to be some flexibility because some situations are going to require one strategy well other situations require a different strategy.

Taking Too Much Risk

If you noticed with the strategies that we examined, there are some trade-offs that have to be made. The trade-offs often involve a trade-off between the amount of profit you can make and the level of risk. People are always greedy I can guarantee that, but one thing that really does is get you into trouble when it comes to trading. You need to be disciplined and methodical. So that means not taking too much risk when it can be avoided. It's better to seek small profits in small bites that can add up rather than trying to hit a home run.

Set It and Forget It

This is a huge mistake the beginners make. They think buying an option is a cool idea, and so they buy an option. But then they don't spend every day studying it and following it. Maybe they hear on the news that the stock drop by five dollars. Then if they go to check their option, they might find that it lost $65 in value. Don't ever take to set it and forget it approach. Every option that you trade, you need to pay attention to in detail every day.

Forgetting About Time Decay

Time decay is one of the most important properties of options. Every day an option is losing extrinsic or time value. But some people leave their options for a long time hoping that the stock is going to move in a favorable direction. Then it never does and they end up losing money when the option expires worthless. So you have to keep in mind that an option has time decay and that the option is going to lose value because of this. If it's not in the money, that means it's losing value overall.

When Selling Options, Stop Looking at Probabilities

One thing that can also be tempting is to always aim for the highest premium that you can earn when selling a credit spread. That is a bad strategy. Even though you might get a large credit, you might also put yourself in a high risk of assignment. The goal should be to set up trades that have a high probability of success. Would you rather have a trade that might make $200 but it has a 65% chance of failure, or would you rather have a trade that made $75 and had a 95% chance of success? I think it's the latter that would appeal to most people. The thing is the $75 is just one trade. You can do 10 or 20 of those trades.

Not Paying Attention to Volatility

Every time you look up an option I advise you to look at the implied volatility. This is actually an estimate of the future volatility of the stock that underlies the option. If the implied volatility is high that means higher option prices generally speaking. If you're selling options, you are going to want to sell options where the implied volatility is higher. That is something that a lot of people ignore, once again beginner seems to only focus on the price they receive for the option.

Not Having a Training Plan

Besides setting general goals, you should have a trading plan in place. The first part of your training plan would be to establish how much money you're willing to risk on every trade. Another thing to look at is what strategy are you going to use to determine which trades to enter? For example, you might just do it on a whim when it seems like the stock is going up. In fact, that's how most people view the markets. but you could take a different approach instead of doing that what you could do is have a technical analysis based reason to enter a trade. For example, if the stock price has been dropping but then there's a golden cross which means that a short period moving average has crossed over on top of the lawn. Moving average, this is a good sign that you should enter a trade. So you could start your week picking out the stocks that you're interested in for that week. I advise working with a small number of stocks at any given time, so you could pick three such as Facebook, Lucky Martin, and Amazon. Then what you do is you studied the charts and wait for the right moment to enter the trade.

Not Giving Enough Time or Even Thinking About Time

It's important to think about the expiration date that you pick when trading options. This needs to be taken into account when you watch the price of the auction going up and down. There is always a possibility that an option it's going down is going to rebound later on if there is a long time until the expiration. So if there was only three days left for an option, and it was losing money, that is a trade that I would definitely say cut your losses. But if there are three weeks left, panicking every time the option goes down in value is a really bad idea. Instead, you need to let it sit there and wait until the right moment to sell it. Even if that means only going so far is breaking even so you can get out of the trade without losing money. But the time left expiration is a very important factor in deciding how to handle that situation.

Conclusion

Thank you for taking the time to read this little book about options. I have done my best to explain options using plain English so that anyone can understand. I hope that this has taken some of the mystery out of options and that you may feel more comfortable in pursuing a career trading them or just trading options on the side.

Options are often portrayed as being extremely risky, but they are only risky if you trade blind. In fact, options don't really carry that much. If you are foolish and let options that you buy head right into expiration without selling them off, or when a stock is in an obvious downward trend but you hold on to your call options bet that went bad, then I suppose that options are really risky. But for those that take the time to learn about it and study the concept carefully, trading options should not be that complicated or risky.

There are many different strategies that can be employed. Remember, however, that to use them you are going to have to get the appropriate trader level designation. Once you do, then you can use options to do amazing things that stock traders simply cannot do. Your friends with mutual funds will be grumbling when the stock market is crashing, but you will be smiling because you will be using the strategies outlined in this book in order to earn big profits from the downturn. Then when it reverses course you will return to your normal way of trading, and continue to make money.

Please don't stop with this book. You should continue studying and learning so that you can be a successful trader.

If you have found this book to be helpful, I'd appreciate a constructive review.

www.ingramcontent.com/pod-product-compliance
Lightning Source LLC
Chambersburg PA
CBHW070347220526
45467CB00001B/284